Ripley's Believe It or Not!®

Special Edition 2013

SCHOLASTIC INC.

New York   Toronto   London   Auckland
Sydney   Mexico City   New Delhi   Hong Kong

ISBN 978-0-545-43505-5

RIPLEY
PUBLISHING

Developed and produced by Ripley Publishing Ltd

Publisher: Anne Marshall
Editorial Director: Becky Miles
Art Director: Sam South

Project Editor: Rosie Alexander
Assistant Editor: Charlotte Howell
Senior Researcher: James Proud
Design: Rocket Design (East Anglia) Ltd
Indexer: Hilary Bird
Reprographics: Juice Creative

Cover credits:
Photography by Glen La Ferman
Art Direction by Rick DeMonico
Digital composition by Rob Kolb

12 11 10 9 8 7 6 5 4 3 2 1   12 13 14 15 16 17/0

Printed in China
First Printing, September 2012   82

See page 23

See page 121

Contents

See page 45

See page 128

See page 106

The Ripley Hunt Is On ...

Life-sized statue

Like a hound on a trail, Ripley's identifies, pursues, and pounces on extraordinary tales and pictures from around the globe. In Ripley's massive organization, there are researchers and correspondents, explorers and investigators—all ready to react to a tip-off that enters Ripley's offices via e-mail, the Web site, mail, Facebook, Twitter, Ripley's TV and radio shows, or as an unspoken nod and a wink.

The great Robert Ripley would have approved. He began his mission to reveal the world's most unbelievably true stories in 1918, when he worked as a cartoonist at *The New York Globe*. Concentrating at first on "Believe It or Not!" achievements in athletics, he soon broadened his search to include the rest of mankind. He traveled over 464,000 miles in his lifetime, and collected material wherever he went. His readers supported his enthusiasm—in one two-week period in 1932, he received over 2 million letters, each one containing a peculiar tale.

Robert Ripley became a huge star. When he died in 1949, thousands lined the streets of New York to watch his coffin pass by. Today, the Ripley collection includes 25,000 artifacts, 25,000 photos, and 100,000 cartoons. At least that was the figure when this book went to press. Ripley's fans have since been in touch....

This statue of Arnold Schwarzenegger as the Terminator was created by Mexican artist Enrique Ramos and was acquired by Ripley's in 2011. It's a tribute to Hollywood films and stars, so it contains tiny images of Spider-Man, Homer Simpson, E.T., Jaws, and Frankenstein's monster. There is even a dead bat. See how many you can spot.

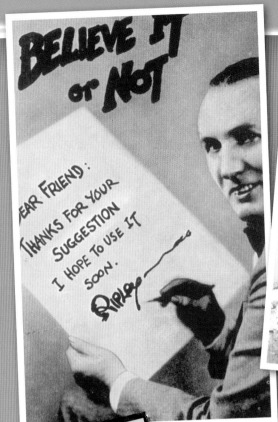

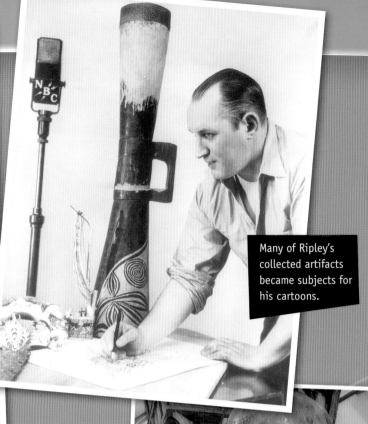

Many of Ripley's collected artifacts became subjects for his cartoons.

FOUND and purchased by Ripley's recently...

Replica elephant inside

Giant portraits of Bill and Hillary Clinton painted with **hamburger grease**.

Five flags **flown on the Moon** during *Apollo* space missions.

An 18th-century Indo-Persian suit of **elephant armor** (center right) that would have carried important warriors into battle in India.

An interpretation of Leonardo da Vinci's *The Last Supper* made from **laundry lint**.

Michael Jackson's plaster fangs from the **"Thriller"** video.

Harry Potter's Hogwarts Castle, made from **matchsticks**, and a whole matchstick Minas Tirith city from *Lord of the Rings*.

Elvis Presley's black eyeliner makeup kit.

A **licorice** motorcycle.

Ten robot Transformers made from car-body parts, (right). They were built in Bangkok, Thailand, and now stand in Ripley's museums around the world, including London, England and San Antonio, Texas.

8 feet tall

CLOSE UP

Follow the clues to spot the story under the microscope.

The real Lizardman!

Reptile Replica

The art department at Ripley's Florida HQ makes model copies of the most amazing "Believe It or Not!" characters. Lizardman, Erik Sprague from Austin, Texas, is one. He has transformed himself into a creature, part-man part-reptile. His body is completely covered in scaly tattoos, nobbly implants poke from his forehead, his tongue is forked, and his teeth are filed to a point. To get his shape truly accurate, Erik's entire body was first covered in silicone and plaster to make a mold. Then a resin figure was produced and painted to form an incredible likeness.

What a weird, wild world...

It's the end of life as you know it! You've opened this book and BANG! In that second, you've been made aware that while most people happily plod along with their day-to-day business, our planet is jam-packed with people and places that really make life fizz. The world is bustling and busy with incredible inventions, curious critters, fabulous facts, and magical miracles. Hundreds of them wait on the following pages and they'll get you gasping and grimacing —and everything else in between.

See page 78

See page 127

See page 35

JUICY BIT
These bite-sized bits of information will leave you with something to chew on.

Turn to pages 42–43 and 130–131 and pore over fantastic old black-and-white photos taken from the Ripley archive. The archive is a vast photographic source that collects together Robert Ripley's own photographs and those sent to him over the years. Ripley often used the photographs as reference for his newspaper cartoons. The "Believe It or Not!" cartoons are still produced today on a daily basis.

chapter 1

Out of this World

It's Only Natural

Luminous Lakes

A ghostly, blue glow illuminated the waters of Australia's Gippsland Lakes at night during 2008. A mix of forest fires and torrential rain had created the perfect conditions for *Noctiluca scintillans*, also known as "sea sparkle." This microorganism uses bioluminescence as a defense mechanism. After sensing a predator, the microorganism lights up, which attracts an even larger predator! Now the second, larger predator can eliminate the first predator and the microorganism avoids being eaten.

Graciela's Guitar

Argentinian farmer Pedro Martin Ureta created this giant, green guitar using 7,000 cypress and eucalyptus trees as a tribute to his late wife, Graciela. She first came up with the idea after seeing a farm that looked like a milking pail from above, and after planting and pruning the trees, Mr. Ureta and his family have maintained the guitar shape ever since. Pilots stare in amazement at Mr. Ureta's memorial, but he has never seen it from the air because he's afraid of flying.

Colorful Crop

Each May, the fields of northern Holland explode into a riot of color as over three billion tulips bloom. This rainbow carpet quickly disappears when the flowers are picked for sale around the world. In the 1630s, Holland was gripped by "tulipmania," when the plant became a status symbol and some bulbs exchanged hands for more than the cost of a house.

Carved by Nature

The spectacular rock formations in Joshua Tree National Park, California, are the result of millions of years of weathering during a period when this desert region was cooler and wetter than today. Wind and rain have sculpted the massive granite boulders into extraordinary shapes, including a skull and this elephant-shaped rock.

JUICY BIT
In 1811, one of the most powerful earthquakes in human history struck in Missouri and caused a tsunami in the Mississippi River, making it run backward for several hours.

Like Nothing on Earth

Dry Falls

In 1969, the U.S. Army dammed the Niagara River so they could strengthen the riverbed to delay the erosion of the rock. The 60,000 gallons of water that normally flow down Niagara Falls every second were diverted over the Horseshoe Falls in Canada. Photographs of the dry falls surfaced 41 years later and show a barren cliff face instead of the usual mass of water.

Pretty in Pink

A high concentration of minerals and microorganisms give Lake Retba in the African country of Senegal a beautiful rosy color, which ranges from deep pink to purple. The waters of this shallow lagoon contain up to eight times more salt than the sea. Local people collect the water from boats, or by wading in, and harvest the salt by letting the sparkling white heaps evaporate on the shore.

JUICY BIT

A trail of light once spotted in the night sky above North America was not a shooting star, but a batch of astronauts' urine, dumped from the space shuttle Discovery.

Supersize Spillway

When California's Lake Berryessa fills to capacity, excess water spills over into this massive funnel, which measures 72 feet at its widest point. The drain swallows water at a rate of 362,000 gallons a second and carries it 700 feet to the bottom of the Monticello Dam, 300 feet below. Buoys keep swimmers and boaters away, in case they might be foolish enough to try and ride the giant flume. The horizontal exit pipe attracts hardcore BMX riders and skateboarders during the dry season.

Shhlurrp!

CLOSE UP

Look closer on page 104 to figure this one out.

Under the Weather

Colorful Cloud

Astronomer Oleg Bartunov expected to enjoy some spectacular views during his expedition to the Himalayas in Nepal, but this rainbow cloud took him by surprise. He spotted the cloud, which some say looks like a reclining angel, hovering above Mount Everest, the world's highest mountain. This rare phenomenon occurs when sunlight reflects off tiny ice crystals in the cloud.

Celestial Alphabet

Danièle Siebenhaar was inspired to compile a cloud alphabet after noticing the letter L in the sky. Her passion for clouds began when she was looking for a photo for a concert program and spotted a cloud that looked like a grand piano. Since then, the 71-year-old from Zurich, Switzerland, has snapped many pictures of oddly shaped clouds, including a dinosaur, a surfer, and a sleeping baby.

What do the clouds spell?

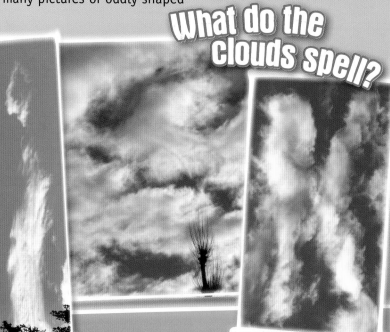

Ice House

You might expect to find the White Witch of Narnia living in this fairy-tale castle, but beneath the multiple layers of ice lies the Cleveland Harbor West Pierhead Lighthouse, on the shores of Lake Erie. High winds caused waves to crash onto the building, and the water froze in the subzero temperatures, turning the building into an ice palace.

JUICY BIT

"Lady Liberty" has a four-foot-six-inch-long nose, her index finger measures over eight feet, and one of her fingernails is 13 by 10 inches. To climb to the top of her crown you have to take the 354 steps!

Lucky Strike

Jay Fine captured the shot of a lifetime when a huge bolt of lightning struck the Statue of Liberty in September 2010. The New York photographer had waited for almost two hours and taken more than 80 shots before he struck luck with this dramatic image. The 305-foot-tall statue is thought to be hit by lightning about 600 times a year.

Flash Facts

A bolt of lightning can reach a peak temperature of 55,000°F. That's about five times hotter than the surface of the Sun.

A typical lightning bolt has a circumference as small as a U.S. quarter, but the bright light makes it look wider.

There are about 16 million lightning storms in the world every year, and lightning strikes the ground between 30 and 100 times every second.

And the Zip Code Is ...

Heavens Above!

Intrepid churchgoers may feel closer to heaven once they have climbed the rickety ladder up to the ancient church near Chiatura, in the former Soviet republic of Georgia. The church, which perches on a narrow pillar of rock 130 feet above the ground, is home to Father Maxim, who has been preaching from on high for many years.

Cracking Idea

Dai Haifei couldn't afford to shell out for an apartment when he found a job in China's capital, Beijing, so the 24-year-old built his own egg-shaped home for $1,000. Dai's eco-pod is insulated with burlap sacks filled with sawdust and grass seed, which he waters daily to make the grass grow. A solar panel and rechargeable battery power the lights and an electric blanket.

Shed of Dreams

While most sheds hold garden tools and old pots of paint, Paul Siudowski's backyard hideaway in South Wales is fitted with a 16-foot-long bar, a jukebox, and popcorn and jellybean machines. Paul created his diner-style shed to house his collection of 1950s American memorabilia. The extended outhouse can seat 24 people and has been entered in the Shed of the Year competition.

All the Tea in China

It's hard to miss the Museum of Tea Culture in Meitan, China. The 240-foot-tall teapot building, which stands alongside a matching teacup, could hold over 7,563 gallons of tea—enough to fill 158,823 cups. The monument celebrates China's long history of tea drinking which, according to legend, dates back to 2737 BC, when tea leaves blew into Emperor Shen Nung's cup of hot water.

Anyone for a cup of tea?

Road Rage-ous

Sticky Situation

A recently laid road in Zhengzhou melted when a heat wave swept through China in July 2010. As the mercury rose to over 100°F, the temperature of the road surface hit 158°F, and the asphalt turned to a gluey consistency. The asbestos cloth laid beneath the tarmac became wrapped around vehicles' wheels, and a taxi and an ambulance almost collided after getting tangled in the same length of cloth.

Hot!

Crazy Cargo

Konstanty Krol and Cezar Chmielewski had more than a spare tire in the back of their van. When German police stopped the pair because their vehicle was lurching from side to side, they were amazed to find a car wedged inside. The men, from Kazakhstan, had squeezed a Mazda 626 into the van to transport it home and save on the cost of a trailer.

3-D Deterrent

Traffic-safety officials in West Vancouver, British Columbia, Canada, came up with an unusual way to deter motorists from speeding in a school zone. The week-long experiment featured an elongated image of a girl chasing a ball. It looked flat from most angles, but as drivers approached, the optical illusion appeared to rise up from the road.

JUICY BIT

James Faulkner has designed a range of hats made from roadkill. The milliner's macabre materials include fur and feathers from flattened magpies, rabbits, pheasants, mallards, and pigeons.

Soft Top Sedan

Parking attendants in Clerkenwell, London, must have been bemused by this life-sized Chevrolet Orlando made entirely of Play-Doh. It took a team of eight model makers two weeks to sculpt the car using 1.4 tons of the modeling putty (the equivalent of 10,000 pots). The car cost $10,000 to make, about one-third the price of the real thing, and caused a shortage of aquamarine Play-Doh across Europe.

Playful Planet

Blue Boulders

In 1984, Belgian artist Jean Verame teamed up with a group of Moroccan firefighters to create this dramatic piece of art in the Anti-Atlas Mountains near Tafraoute. It took them three months to spray the boulders and low hills with 20 tons of blue, red, violet, and white paint. The colors are fading now, but the blend of art and nature is still striking.

CLOSE UP

Which animal has high expectations? See page 79.

Cappuccino Coastline

Surfers in Yamba, Australia, got a shock when the ocean turned into a giant bubble bath. Powerful currents and wild weather whipped organic matter, including dead plants, plankton, and decomposing fish, into a thick layer of froth. The clouds of cappuccino-like foam buried the shoreline and stretched 165 feet out into the Pacific Ocean.

Giant Firepit

Darvaza, Turkmenistan, is rich in natural gas. When the ground beneath a drilling rig collapsed in 1971, geologists decided to burn off the gas that was escaping from the 200-foot-wide crater. They expected the fire to go out after a few days but, more than 40 years later, it is still burning. No one knows how much gas remains in the 65-foot-deep hole, which has since become a tourist attraction.

JUICY BIT

The Paricutin Volcano in Mexico began as a crack in a cornfield in 1943, and grew to the height of a five-story building within a week! By the end of the year it was a mountain, standing 1,102 feet tall.

BIG SHOT

Awesome Ape

Dutch artist Florentijn Hofman created this huge ape, called "Fat Monkey," for the city of São Paulo's Pixel Show in Brazil. The giant inflatable is covered with more than 10,000 pairs of flip-flops, each shoe representing one pixel. Local students helped dress the creature in Brazil's iconic footwear of choice. The artist is well-known for his oversized animals. His floating rubber ducks, some 85 feet tall, have towered above boats in harbors around the world, and he filled a gallery in The Hague, Netherlands, with enormous stuffed toys.

He's flopped!

"Let's Talk"

Florentijn, why do you love enormous animals?
They make the world smaller. They say a lot about the perspective between objects and space.

What happened to all the flip-flops after the sculpture was dismantled?
We gave them away to passing spectators and people who were living and working in the vicinity of the work.

What will your next big work be?
I am working on the Kobe Frog, a frog on the roof of the Hyogo Prefectural Museum of Art in Kobe, Japan. Besides this, I am working on a mascot for the city of Aalst in Belgium.

Globe-trotting

Tiny Terminal

Planes take off into the clouds, tow trucks maneuver around the runways, and passengers line up in the terminal. These scenes are repeated at airports around the world, but Knuffingen Airport is different. It is the latest exhibit at Miniatur Wunderland in Hamburg, Germany, and the whole airport could fit in your basement. The model took seven years to build and cost about $4.8 million.

JUICY BIT

A passenger in a South African air force display plane accidentally pulled a lever activating the ejection seat and was propelled 300 feet into the air! An automatic parachute carried him safely down to Earth.

QT RV

Trailers and RVs are known for hogging the highway, but this pint-sized travel trailer is more suited to the sidewalk. Designed to be towed by a scooter or a bicycle, the QTvan contains a bed, TV, and kettle. It may be perfect for a "staycation" close to home, but not ideal for a long-haul trip, because its top speed is just six miles per hour.

The Great Indoors

Part of an old vacuum cleaner factory has been converted into a hotel where guests sleep in old caravans and wooden huts. The Hüttenpalast (Hut Palace) Hotel in Berlin, Germany, even has a garden with hanging wash lines. The huts and caravans have been customized by local artists, and residents can enjoy breakfast sitting outside them as if they were on a real camping vacation.

Don't Look Down!

Instead of having to peer through tiny airplane portholes, future fliers can look forward to a 360-degree window on the world, with amazing views of the night sky. A concept airliner unveiled by Airbus has a see-through cabin with holographic, pop-up gaming displays, and in-flight entertainment powered by the heat from passengers' bodies. It could be taking off from an airport near you in 2050.

Ripley's @ a glance

BIG BRIDGE

China has opened a 26.4-mile-long sea bridge, supported by 5,000 pillars. The sweeping Y-shaped bridge across Jiaozhou Bay, Shandong Province, cost $1.5 billion to build, and it is predicted that 30,000 cars will cross it each day.

GREAT WHITE ICE

If you're bored by Cherry Garcia and Dublin Mudslide, how about shark fin, whale, or octopus ice cream? Take a trip to Japan and you could enjoy these and other flavors, including beef tongue, pit viper, and basashi, which contains raw horsemeat.

SMOOTH RIDE

Following passenger complaints about bad driving and sudden stops, a Chinese bus company has suspended bowls of water in the drivers' cabs to make sure they drive smoothly. The bowls must still be full when the drivers finish work and closed-circuit television ensures that they do not top them up with water.

HOME RICH HOME

The wealthiest man in India now owns the world's most expensive single family home. Indian billionaire Mukesh Ambani and the four other members of his family have moved into their 1-billion-dollar home, called Antilla, in downtown Mumbai.

WHAT HE GETS FOR HIS MONEY...

- 398,265 square feet (it's bigger than the Palace of Versailles)
- 27 stories
- 3 helicopter landing pads on the roof
- Garage with space for 160 cars
- 9 elevators
- A staff of 600
- Panoramic view of the Arabian Sea from the top floor
- An electricity bill for the first month of 7 million rupees ($156,000)

FRAGRANT FOOD

A restaurant in Argentina has invented a new cuisine called "Pop Food," which includes designer perfumes. Sifones y Dragones serves dishes such as oysters with Anaïs Anaïs, Chanel No. 5 ice cream, and chocolate mousse with raw ham and Jean Paul Gaultier's Le Male scent.

FIRE FRIGHT

When firefighters tackling a blaze at a Pittsburgh hotel came across a blood-spattered room, they called the police. Police Chief J.R. Blyth said it was the worst murder scene he'd encountered in his 35 years in law enforcement, before realizing that the blood was fake. The hotel owner then explained that the room had been the set for a horror movie shot at the hotel.

SPOOKY SALE

With a population of just 35, Cuchillo, New Mexico, is a virtual ghost town, and resident Josh Bond has offered what he claims to be a genuine haunted house for sale on eBay. The auction ended, appropriately enough, on Halloween.

TO HAVE AND TO SWIM WITH

Sharon Tendler married Cindy the dolphin in a special ceremony in Eilat, Israel, in 2005. After saying, "I do," Sharon knelt down to give Cindy a kiss and a piece of wedding herring. They first met 15 years ago, but Cindy sadly passed away just one year after their wedding in 2006.

HAPPY (MEAL) EVER AFTER

Couples in Hong Kong can say "I do" under the golden arches (and avoid arguments over seating plans) by celebrating their wedding at McDonald's. A McWedding package includes the ceremony, reception, wedding cake, and catering for up to 100 people for a bargain price of $400.

CINDY

Street Life

"Ahoy"

Dress-up Dad

Dale Price's 15-year-old son was embarrassed when his dad waved him off to school one day, so his father decided to raise the stakes. The following day, Dale, from Utah, stood at the door wearing an Elvis costume. He continued to dress up each day for the rest of the school year, seeing his son off in a total of 170 outfits, including a mermaid, a pirate (pictured), and a clown.

JUICY BIT

In 2010, workers trying to clear blockage in the sewers beneath London's Leicester Square removed 907 tons of putrid fat—enough to fill nearly nine double-decker buses.

City Solstice

While British druids celebrate the summer solstice among the ancient stones of Stonehenge, New Yorkers look forward to Manhattanhenge, when the city's east-west-lying streets perfectly frame the setting sun. This solar event occurs for two days in late May and again in mid-July. There is a similar phenomenon in winter when the sun rises in line with the skyscraper corridors.

Bone-Chiller

A snowy drain cover in his hometown of Kampen inspired Dutch artist Cem Ulucan to create this piece of street art titled *Cold as Ice*. An accompanying video shows the skeleton moving its head from side to side, then opening the drain cover with one hand to release a red balloon, which can be seen beneath the grid.

Reptilian Ride

Jim Jablon from Florida came up with an unusual raffle prize to raise funds for his wildlife rehabilitation center. He covered a custom-made motorbike with the skin of an alligator, donated by state officials. Although the skin is removable, the head is fixed to the toothy two-wheeler, which has the speedometer implanted into the back of the skull. The winning ticket was plucked from a pool full of gators.

chapter 2

Just Do It!

Danger Zones

Fiery Photos

Most people run away from an erupting volcano, but photographer Skarphedinn Thrainsson headed straight for the crater. The Icelandic daredevil risked being burned by lava, struck by lightning, and hit by chunks of volcanic ash as he captured nature's dramatic fireworks display during the eruption of the Fimmvorduhals and Eyjafjallajokull volcanoes on Iceland's south coast.

Bliinggg!

Blue Grotto

Roger Hiorns took an abandoned London apartment and created a piece of art. The British artist sealed up the apartment, then filled it with 20,000 gallons of copper sulfate solution, a blue chemical often used as a fungicide. During the following weeks, the copper sulfate crystallized on the surfaces of the disused dwelling, turning it into a stunning, blue crystal cavern.

JUICY BIT

Ludwig Fichte solved a Rubik's Cube in 31.5 seconds while sitting in a rubber dinghy in free fall from a plane 14,000 feet above the ground. The German skydiver fell to 3,609 feet before deploying his parachute.

Death-defying Diver

Equipped with nothing more than a flashlight and a monofin, free diver Carlos Coste swam 492 feet through a flooded cave system. The 34-year-old Venezuelan is able to hold his breath for seven minutes, but he needed just 152 seconds to make his way through the winding tunnel inside Dos Ojos, a twisting cave network beneath the Yucatán Peninsula in Mexico. Carlos laid a rope along the route before the dive and used his flashlight to follow it through the pitch-black passage.

"Let's Talk"

Carlos, what were you thinking as you swam through the dark in that cave?
I was focusing on following my diving line above me, relaxing, and keeping my swim rhythm through the cave path. I had to prepare myself to manage the curves in my way, keeping on the line. Positive thoughts all the way!

Can you tell us some of the special techniques you use in free diving?
Complete yoga breathing, visualization, double kick with gliding monofin technique, and a lot of training in the pool, gym, and sea. But the most important thing is attitude—positive, of course—knowing yourself step by step, and good relaxation.

Did the dive in Mexico require much planning?
Yes. We were planning it for a year, but the idea of doing it came up three years ago. We made two trips to explore different possible cenotes [sinkholes]. The support team was led by Gaby Contreras, my wife, along with an international team from Mexico, Venezuela, France, Spain, and the U.K. The team made it possible and safe.

Going the Distance

Purely Pink

Many girls grow out of their passion for pink, but not actress Kitten Kay-Sera. Known as the Pink Lady, Kitten, who is in her late forties, has dressed in pink for the past 25 years and even wears the color to funerals. Her home is a shrine to the shade and she dyes her Maltese dog, Kisses, with beet juice.

CLOSE UP

Turn to page 127 to solve this puzzle!

Birthday Briefs

Jack Singer celebrated his tenth birthday by pulling on 215 pairs of underpants weighing more than 30 pounds. It took the fourth grader from Warwick, New York, 18 minutes to don the tighty whities in ever-increasing sizes. Jack needed his family's help to pull on the layers of underwear and had to lie down when they reached 195 pairs because he lost the feeling in his feet.

Tiny Tomes

Dream of the Red Chamber is such an important masterpiece of Chinese literature that an elderly gentleman in Zhengzhou has gone to extreme lengths to ensure he always has a copy. Zhang Enmao has collected 1,250 versions of the book and has even created his own nano-novels, with characters the size of the eye of a needle.

Where's Waldo?

The challenge in Dublin's Merrion Square was to find someone who wasn't Waldo. In June 2011, 3,657 people dressed in red-and-white-striped T-shirts and matching hats, peered at one another through black-rimmed eyeglasses for Ireland's Street Performance World Championship. Dogs even got in on the act, with several Woof lookalikes accompanying their owners.

I'm here!

Tiny Tasks

Mini Marvels

It seems nothing is too small to form the basis of one of Vladimir Aniskin's micro-masterpieces. Inspired by a folktale about a craftsman who shoed a dancing flea, the Russian artist cast his own tiny shoes, each just 0.0019 inches wide, for one of his cat's fleas, while his Christmas scene rests on half a poppy seed.

ПОДКОВАЛ РУССКИЙ МАСТЕР АНИСКИН В.М.

ЯНВАРЬ 2007

БЛОШКА МУСЯ. СПОНСОР – КОТ КУЗЯ.

←ГВОЗДИКИ

С НОВЫМ ГОДОМ!

2006

JUICY BIT

Portuguese company Awaiba has produced a camera for medical use that is smaller than the head of a match. To be used in the medical world for a variety of purposes, NanEye 2B can take clear and sharp pictures.

Compact Cube

If solving a Rubik's Cube is too easy, try tackling Evgeny Grigoriev's miniature version the size of a fingertip. It took the Russian computer programmer a month to design the half-inch cube, which was laser-cut from special plastic. Evgeny can solve a normal puzzle in a minute, but even he needs about five minutes to complete his tiny cube.

Techno-art

Perfect for the geek with a love of art (and excellent eyesight), Yuri Zupancic creates miniature paintings on microchips less than an inch wide. The American artist, who makes some of his brushes from his own eyelashes, was inspired by the phrase "smaller and faster," which is replacing "bigger and better" in today's high-speed world.

Abraham Lincoln 1861–1865

Theodore Roosevelt 1901–1909

John F. Kennedy 1961–1963

Lyndon B. Johnson 1963–1969

Heads on Hair

Perhaps reflecting their positions as "heads" of state, micro-painter Jin Yin Hua has chosen a single human hair just half an inch long as his canvas for this line up of presidential portraits. The Chinese artist has illustrated 42 U.S. presidents, from George Washington to George W. Bush, using a single rabbit hair as a paintbrush.

Lincoln and Kennedy

Abraham Lincoln was elected to Congress in 1846. John F. Kennedy was elected to Congress 100 years later, in 1946.

Lincoln was elected president in 1860. Kennedy was elected president 100 years later, in 1960.

Both presidents were shot in the head and died on a Friday.

Lincoln was assassinated in a theater built by Ford. Kennedy was assassinated in a car built by Ford.

Lincoln's killer, John Wilkes Booth, ran from a theater and was caught in a warehouse. Kennedy's killer, Lee Harvey Oswald, ran from a warehouse and was caught in a theater.

Both presidents were succeeded by men named Johnson. Andrew Johnson was born in 1808 and Lyndon Johnson was born 100 years later, in 1908.

BIG SHOT

Is It a Bus ... Is It a Plane?

Few kids want to get to school faster, but less time on the bus means longer in bed. The journey would fly by in Paul Stender's "School Time Jet-Powered School Bus," which has been fitted with an engine from a Phantom fighter jet. The hot rod reaches a top speed of 367 miles per hour, while belching out 80-foot flames and huge clouds of smoke. The structure of the original bus could never withstand the extreme speeds, so self-taught mechanic Paul has replaced most parts using metals found on an airplane. The yellow bus is far from green, however. It uses a staggering 150 gallons of fuel in one quarter-mile run.

Time Trials

One Way to Wake Up

Morning workouts are a way of life for retired people in China, so a senior exercising in a public park wouldn't normally draw a second glance. However, Xu Tiancheng always attracts a crowd. Xu has practiced kung fu for 30 years, and spending **30 minutes** balanced on his head on top of a nail is part of his regular morning routine.

Ouch!

JUICY BIT

Basketball balancer Bruce Crevier from South Dakota can spin a basketball on one finger nonstop for *22 hours 12 minutes,* including during bathroom breaks. He can also spin 21 basketballs simultaneously.

Human Buoy

S.C. Naganandaswamy from India was already a dedicated swimmer when he read about the technique "aqua trance." This normally involves floating horizontally but Mr. Naganandaswamy was determined to master the skill vertically. He practiced yoga and experimented in local wells and ponds until he achieved his goal of floating vertically without moving his limbs for **22 hours** in 20-foot-deep water.

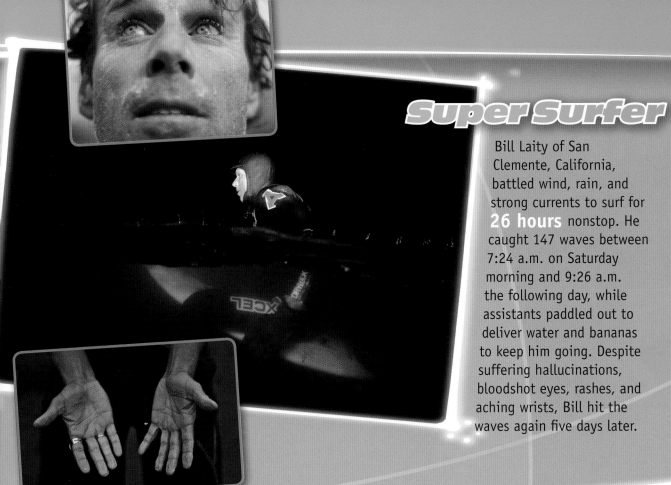

Super Surfer

Bill Laity of San Clemente, California, battled wind, rain, and strong currents to surf for **26 hours** nonstop. He caught 147 waves between 7:24 a.m. on Saturday morning and 9:26 a.m. the following day, while assistants paddled out to deliver water and bananas to keep him going. Despite suffering hallucinations, bloodshot eyes, rashes, and aching wrists, Bill hit the waves again five days later.

Yellow Submarine

French engineer Stephane Rousson pedaled his muscle-powered submarine for **60 minutes** during its test dive in the Mediterranean Sea. Driven by twin propellers connected to a pedal belt, the single-seater Scubster can reach a speed of six miles per hour and dive to a depth of 20 feet. The carbon-fiber sub does not have an on-board oxygen supply, so the pilot has to wear full scuba gear.

Ripley Revisited

Look, No Feet

Skating tricks have been around as long as roller skates. Here, Peggy Gray of Plainfield, New Jersey, demonstrates how to skate upside down without a half-pipe.

Unusual Unicycle

The height of a unicycle is normally limited by the length of the rider's leg, but this man, Walter Nilsson, is riding a "giraffe"—a unicycle powered by a chain. Giraffe unicycles can be more than ten feet high.

And rinse...

Bar Bender

Most people use special equipment to bend metal rods, but this muscular young woman has found a simpler way to do it—although her dentist may not approve.

THE HUMAN FOUNTAIN

Human Fountain

Mortado the Human Fountain would spray water out of holes that had been made in his hands and feet. Copper pipes were attached to the holes and water from the pipes spurted out, transforming the 1930s sideshow performer into a living fountain.

FORE!

Strong Swing!

In 1935, golf pro Alex Ednie demonstrated the power of a new golf ball by driving it straight through a 500-page phone book at the Shelter Rock Country Club in New York. This feat was even more amazing because the book was standing on its end without any support. The ball kept on traveling for 100 yards after piercing the book, and its initial speed was estimated at 114 miles per hour.

Baby Body Builder

This pocket-sized power lifter is more of a gym rat than a rug rat. The brawny baby may have started training early, but he still has a way to go before he makes the weight.

My, Oh Why?

Balancing Act

Freddy Nock walked more than 5,200 feet down the wire of the Corvatsch cable car near the ski resort of St. Moritz, Switzerland, with nothing but a pole to help him balance. The high-wire artist started his walk at 10,835 feet above sea level. Fearless Freddie comes from a well-known Swiss circus family, and started wire-walking at the age of just four years old.

'Scraper Scaler

In March 2011, French "Spider-Man" Alain Robert climbed the 2,716-foot Burj Khalifa building in Dubai. It took the urban climber just over six hours to scale the tower, including its tricky, tapered spire. Alain started climbing as a boy and honed his skills in the Alps. He has since scaled over 80 giant structures around the world.

JUICY BIT

U.S. motor sport legend Travis Pastrana backflipped his dirt bike over a hovering helicopter in front of Australia's Sydney Harbor Bridge. He cleared the chopper blades, which were spinning at 385 revolutions per minute, by about 13 feet.

Great Escape

"Let's Talk"

Anthony, during the skydive, did you ever think you wouldn't make it?

When I am "in the zone" and in the middle of an escape, I am thinking of nothing but the required tasks that must take place to succeed. Everything is blocked out of my mind, yet I always seem to have an internal clock that knows how much time I have.

How hard was the escape?

The difficulty of a skydiving spin is that the centrifugal force wants to take my eyes off the work I need to do. I can alter the position of my legs to stop the spin, but that requires me to divide my attention (something I don't like to do).

Escape artist Anthony Martin made a death-defying leap while wearing handcuffs from an airplane flying at 13,500 feet. The cuffs were locked to a chain around his neck and connected to leather cuffs above his elbows. Anthony had only 45 seconds to remove the handcuffs and release his parachute, however after just 25 seconds of struggling he managed to unlock the cuffs and deploy the chute. There was no backup plan in case of problems, as the automatic safety device that would have opened his chute at 700 feet was turned off.

Sporting Chance

Log Ride

Onbashira is an ancient Japanese festival that is held every six years to rebuild the Suwa Grand Shrine in Suwa City. Logs weighing up to 12 tons are slid down the mountain to the Shrine location six miles away, while young men prove their bravery by riding the logs down the perilous slopes. When they reach their destination, the logs are then pulled upright and become the pillars of the four buildings that make up the Shrine.

Weeeeeeee

CLOSE UP

Lovable or horrible? Decide on page 109.

Fruitful Experience

Ashrita Furman from New York has an unusual list of achievements, including walking for more than 80 miles with a milk bottle on his head, but he considers pushing an orange along the ground with his nose for a mile one of his most rewarding experiences. He performed this extraordinary feat in 24 minutes 36 seconds at JFK Airport, much to the amazement of stunned passengers.

Sub-aqua Sprinter

In 2003, Wolfgang Kulow combined his love of diving and running by completing an underwater marathon. He wore a belt containing two 88-pound lead weights and size 16 sneakers over his diving suit. The endurance test was held in a swimming pool near his home in Germany and took 24 hours, 24 minutes to finish. In 2009, he also got married underwater.

JUICY BIT

Jesus Leonardo from New Jersey earns $45,000 a year by picking up discarded betting slips and cashing in winning tickets thrown away by mistake.

Tough Teeth

Michael Chukwuma is said to have the strongest teeth in Africa. The gym instructor and decorator from Lagos, Nigeria, can lift weights up to 330 pounds, pull cars, and carry bags of rice and cement using just his teeth. He started by carrying a dumbbell rod in his mouth and gradually adding weights to it.

Ripley's @ a glance

NO SPRING CHICKEN

When Les and Beryl Lailey got married in 1956, one of their gifts was a food hamper containing a cooked chicken in a tin. The Laileys put the chicken away in a cupboard and Les promised that he would eat it on their 50th wedding anniversary. He bit into the chicken in 2006, declaring it quite tasty but a bit salty.

SCARY SEQUEL

Indian director Ram Gopal Varma has offered a prize of 500,000 rupees to anyone who can watch the sequel to his horror movie *Phoonk* alone in an empty movie theater without getting frightened. An ECG machine, connected to a screen outside the hall, will monitor the contestant's heart rate.

HOLY TRASH

Since 1961, former monk Justo Martinez has devoted his life to building a cathedral single-handedly. The impressive structure, in a village near Madrid, Spain, is almost entirely constructed from salvaged materials, such as the oil drums he used for the pillars.

MAKE WAY FOR DUCKLINGS

During the 1928 Olympics, Australian rower Henry Pearce pulled up his oars to allow a family of ducks to pass in front of his boat. Even though he was overtaken by his French opponent, Pearce went on to win the race.

FAMILY FEAT

Reverend Dr. Kevin Fast and his son Jacob Fast, 18, celebrated an unconventional Father's Day in June 2011 when they pulled two fire trucks together at the same time. Together the trucks weighed around 150,000 pounds, but the strong-man duo from Canada managed to pull them 100 feet along the street in just 38 seconds.

ICE BREAKER

In 2009, black belt martial artist Chad Netherland smashed 16 blocks of ice, 12 feet high and weighing 1,200 pounds, with a single strike of his bare hand.

DARING DIVE

Chinese cliff diver Di Huanran performed a 40-foot dive from the top of the Diaoshuilou Waterfall into Jingpo Lake, northeast China.

SPEED IS OF THE ESSENCE

There's no room for time-wasters in this list of amazing achievers.

Jemal Tkeshelashvili from the Republic of Georgia can inflate a hot-water bottle with his nose until the bottle bursts in just 13 seconds.

Czech illusionist, magician, and escapologist Zdenek Bradác can juggle three balls so fast he managed 339 catches in 60 seconds.

Bill Kathan, from Prescott, Arizona, hiked 24 miles across the Grand Canyon from rim to rim in 15 hours and 23 minutes—walking backward all the way.

In his first speed-eating competition, 17-year-old John Davis beat 30 competitors by gobbling a pound of haggis in just two minutes. Haggis, Scotland's national dish, is made of minced sheep's heart, liver, and lungs mixed with onion, mutton fat, and spices, then boiled in a sheep's stomach for three hours.

Eduard Saakashvili can type the English alphabet from A to Z on an iPad in just 5.26 seconds. The 15-year-old son of the Georgian president trained for months to achieve this finger-busting feat.

TITANIC TENNIS CHAMP

Richard Norris Williams survived the sinking of the *Titanic* in 1912 by clinging to a life raft, but his legs were so badly damaged by the freezing water that a doctor wanted to amputate them. Richard refused and went on to win a gold medal in the tennis mixed doubles at the 1924 Olympics.

SHOT DOWN

Chris Wilson thought he had sold the Harrier jump jet he listed on eBay for $110,102...but the buyer was revealed to be a seven-year-old boy, who had accidentally hit the "Buy It Now" button on his dad's account. The aircraft was relisted and the price soared to $147,811—the sale bombed again when eBay decided the jet was a dangerous weapon and withdrew it.

GREAT LAKE SWIMMER

Canadian teacher Paula Stephanson became only the second person in history to swim across all five Great Lakes when she completed her 25-hour, 35-mile swim across Lake Michigan in 2009. She started by crossing Lake Ontario in 1996, at the age of 17.

Risky Business

Alpine Off-roading

Rally driver and professional skier Guerlain Chicherit teamed his twin talents when he put his Mini ALL4 through its paces in his hometown of Tignes, in the French Alps. The modified rally car "skied" down an icy flight of steps and "snowboarded" along a rail slide, then performed a series of tight turns on a frozen lake. The car is also able to jump a 100-foot gap.

Bridge Swallows Truck

Lu Hin escaped with only a broken leg and minor head injuries when his truck loaded with steel dropped straight through a bridge across the Yitong River in northeast China. Luckily, the river was almost dry, otherwise the driver and his passenger would have drowned. Mr. Hin, whose truck and load weighed almost 90 tons, had ignored warning signs showing a maximum weight limit of 14 tons.

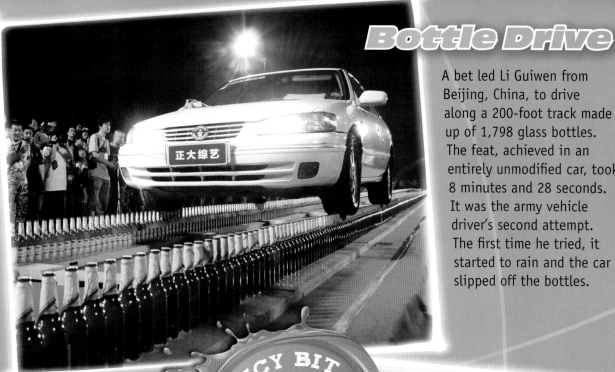

Bottle Drive

A bet led Li Guiwen from Beijing, China, to drive along a 200-foot track made up of 1,798 glass bottles. The feat, achieved in an entirely unmodified car, took 8 minutes and 28 seconds. It was the army vehicle driver's second attempt. The first time he tried, it started to rain and the car slipped off the bottles.

JUICY BIT

In November 2010, Javier Zapata bounced his bike up the 649 steps of the Piedra del Penol, a giant rock in Guatape, Colombia, in just 43 minutes.

Head for Heights

Hunan Province in southern China is known for its natural beauty but the "spidermen" who are building a 1.8-mile-long path along the sheer face of Shifou Mountain probably don't appreciate the amazing views. The cliff-hanging construction workers are supported by little more than rope harnesses and a narrow ledge as they build the scenic tourist trail 300 feet above the valley. Fortunately, the finished path will have guardrails.

chapter 3

Techno-speak

Body Work

Strange Scents

In keeping with the vampire craze, an Italian company has launched a range of blood-scented perfumes. The scents, named A, B, AB, and O after the various blood groups, all have a metallic hint inspired by the red stuff. Alternatively, if you prefer a more familiar smell, why not try a spritz of bacon-scented fragrance from a Chicago-based perfume company?

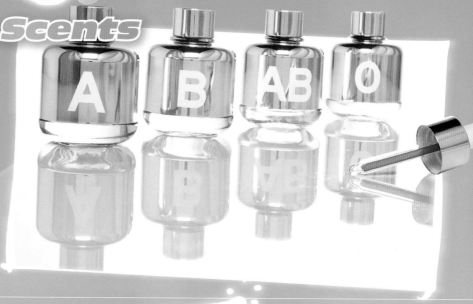

Dazzling Smile

Originally created for a Japanese advertising campaign, LED smiles have become the latest must-have trend. The LED insert, which is described as "a party in your mouth," fixes to the teeth like a mouthguard and can be made to change color and flash using a handheld computer. Now a smile really can light up a room!

Smells good!

Inner Beauty

This striking picture looks like a weird insect or mythical creature, but it is actually part of the human body. Hong Kong radiologist Kai-hung Fung creates beautiful artwork from his patients' CT scans by adding color, using a method he invented called the "rainbow technique." The image shown here is, in fact, the back of the nose.

JUICY BIT

A group of scientists are creating moldy masterpieces by painting on petri dishes using bacteria. The microbial artworks become visible as the bacteria grow, but soon disappear as the bacteria die.

Coat of Invisibility

Harry Potter's Cloak of Invisibility is a step closer to reality thanks to scientists at Tokyo University in Japan. Kazutoshi Obana's "see-through" hooded coat is based on space-age material and camera trickery rather than magic. A video camera behind the wearer is linked to a projector that bounces the image off the front of his coat, which is covered with microscopic reflectors.

Techy Treking

Heli Halo

When particles of dust or sand strike a helicopter's rotor blades they produce static electricity, which appears as a halo of light around the blades at night. War correspondent Michael Yon named this phenomenon the "Kopp-Etchells effect," in honor of U.S. Corporal Benjamin Kopp and British Corporal Joseph Etchells, who were both killed in Afghanistan in 2009.

Print Me a Bike

This fully working bike has been created using the groundbreaking technology of 3-D printing. The Airbike is made of nylon and is as strong as aluminum but weighs 65 percent less. A computer-aided design program splits the 3-D design into 2-D layers, then a special nylon laser printer builds up the made-to-measure bike layer by layer until it is fully formed.

JUICY BIT

American artist Eric Staller's original circular bike for eight riders was intended as a piece of moving artwork, but by reducing the seats to seven, he created the Conference Bike, which is now popular with city tour groups.

Bird Boat

Christian Bohlin must have looked to nature for inspiration when he designed his eye-catching boat. Looking like a toy in a giant bathtub, the Swedish shipbuilder's duck-shaped boat made its debut in Stockholm Harbor in May 2011. The boat contains a sauna, a kitchenette, and two beds, and is expected to sell for about $58,000.

Quackers!

Rainbow Rockets

When a friend remarked that one of his rockets looked like a crayon, inventor John Coker was inspired to produce a Crayola box filled with eight crayon rockets. The rocket enthusiast launched the giant crayons in the Nevada desert, but only four of the eight worked properly. However, he estimated those that did take off shot up to almost 3,000 feet.

Certified Non-Explosive

Crayola

ROCKETS

8

Future Perfect?

Soccer Bot

You can design, build, and program your own robot with the Robotis Bioloid kit from Korea. The Bioloid is seen here being put through its paces at the InnoRobo Summit held in Lyon, France, in 2011. As well as this soccer-playing humanoid, the exhibition showcased more than 100 robots from around the world.

Goal!

Fact File

Science has looked to nature in a new tire that apparently can't go flat. A Wisconsin-based company, Resilient Technologies, has come up with a tire that, instead of using a pressurized air inner tube, relies on a pattern of six-sided cells arranged like a honeycomb.

The D-Box seat is a cinema chair that moves with the action in a film, in an attempt to make movie experiences even more realistic. In addition, speakers have been fitted into the seat, so the sound can be carefully directed for extra atmosphere. A Megaplex in South Jordan, Utah, is one of the first movie theaters to try the seat out.

Zeal Optics have developed ski goggles that are laden with GPS technology and sensors that calculate your speed and altitude as you fly over the snow.

Digital Debit

Imagine being able to go shopping without taking your wallet. Supermarket chains around the world are testing a system that allows customers to pay using just their fingerprints. Shoppers who have registered for the plan simply place a finger on the scanner and the money is automatically taken from their bank account. The technology is also being used in school cafeterias to speed up the lunch lines. Unlike lunch money or pre-payment cards, kids don't normally misplace or forget their fingers.

A yummy strawberry milkshake or not? Flick to page 12.

cLOSE UP

Flexible Phone

Scientists in Canada have created a cell phone as thin and flexible as a sheet of paper. The PaperPhone does everything that a smartphone can, including making and receiving calls, texting, storing books, and playing music. The gadget performs different functions when it is bent, flexed, or folded: for example, bending transforms it into a cell phone, and flipping the corner turns pages.

Contacts

John Buxton
Bill Greenberg
Ravin Grudin
Melody Jacob
Emily Mackay
Ori Miller
Mary Tan

JUICY BIT

Sound is a form of energy and, in theory, if you yelled nonstop for 8 years, 7 months, and 6 days you could produce enough energy to heat a cup of coffee. But it might be easier to use a microwave.

BIG SHOT

Making a Splash

Corrie White, originally from The Netherlands but now living in Canada, uses macrophotography to capture the moment when a tiny droplet falls into a liquid. She usually works with milk or water. Milk

Kersplosh!

falls more slowly than water, allowing her extra milliseconds to snap a perfect shot of the moment of contact. Corrie introduces a thickener called guar gum to water. This slows the water down and creates a smoother shape. A couple of drops of rinse aid helps break the surface tension of the water in the drip tray, allowing the water to move more smoothly.

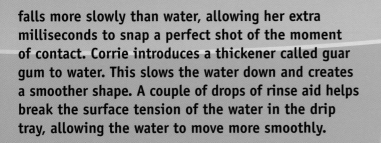

"Let's Talk"

Corrie, isn't getting the perfect photograph just a question of chance?

I use Mumford's Time Machine, which makes things a whole lot easier. With this, I will set how close together the drops fall, the size of the drop of water, and the time I want the flashes to fire to take the picture of the splash. The flash is what freezes the drop. If I set it too early, I may get only a drop in midair and if I set it too late, the water drop will have disappeared into the water in the tray.

Tell us how it's done.

To make a water drop shaped like an umbrella or mushroom, you need to use two drops of water very close together. The first one falls into the water and comes up to form a column. If the second drop of water is close enough, it will fall on the top of this column and spread out to make a nice rounded shape with little tiny droplets around the edge of it.

Corrie first tried a turkey baster, then a medicine dropper, to create the droplets. Now she uses a special drip kit.

Recreation Creations

No Neck Ache

Periscope glasses mean it's possible to read or watch TV in bed without straining your neck or propping your head up on piles of pillows. These glasses bend light through 90 degrees and would be perfect when lying on the beach or lounging in a hammock. Or you could use them to keep an eye on your feet when you're walking.

Dive Detector

Soccer players who pretend they have been kicked unfairly by opposing players could soon be exposed by shin guards that have sensors to detect physical contact. If a player kicks another an alarm will sound, and the referee will decide whether a foul has been committed. Players will not be able to cheat by kicking themselves because the sensor will indicate whether an opponent was close by.

Comfort Station Consoles

Visiting the restroom could be more fun (for men, at least) in the future. Sega is testing urinals linked to video game screens in four Tokyo subway stations. The "Toylets" encourage users to stay on target by hitting a sensor in the bowl that controls the game. Players proud of their achievements can even download their scores onto a USB stick.

JUICY BIT

In a standard pack of playing cards, the king of hearts—sometimes called the "suicide king" because he appears to be sticking his sword into his head—is the only king without a mustache.

Vroom Broom

Ten-year-old Julian Danner invented the "devil's-broom" to give a turbo boost to skaters and skateboarders. The motor-assisted device went on display at a trade fair for ideas, inventions, and new products held in Nuremberg, Germany. Whether it proves to be a speedy way to get around, a vehicle for terrestrial Quidditch, or a fast track to the hospital remains to be seen.

Whoosh!

Explain That!

Alien Hotspot

This cell-phone image was snapped by Lu Yan in July 2010, as a diamond-shaped object shot silently across the night sky in Jinan, eastern China. It came to a standstill and hovered briefly, before zooming off again. A few minutes later, it was followed by three jets. The mysterious sighting follows a number of reports of UFOs over the Chinese mainland in recent years.

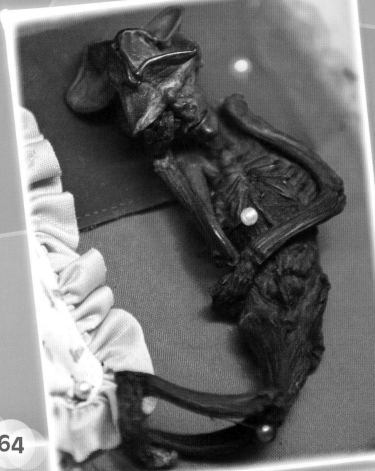

Fruit Fairies

According to Buddhist mythology, the Makalipon tree bears fruit in the form of tiny female fairies. Called Naree Pon, they are said to have appeared as beautiful women to the Buddha. Legend has it that the god Indra planted 16 of the magical trees, one of which is said to grow near the Wat Phra Prang Muni, a temple in Sing Buri Province, Thailand.

CLOSE UP

"Twinkle, twinkle little..." See page 32 for the missing word.

JUICY BIT

In 2011, a strange greenish-yellow goo fell from the skies above Snyder, New York, coating the sidewalks and forming green and yellow icicles on houses. The source of this mysterious substance was never discovered.

Hair-raising Claims

Italian-born Andy Sinatra, known as "The Mystic Barber," had a hair salon in Brooklyn, New York. He claimed to use "astral projection" to visit and communicate with extraterrestrials, and reported that Martians are intelligent cave dwellers, about four feet tall, with blue eyes and white hair. He listened to Mars through an earphone attached to what looked like a transistor radio, and donned an antenna-like headband to sharpen his super senses.

Piano Bar

In 2011, Miami, Florida, residents were mystified when a 650-pound piano suddenly appeared on a sandbar in Biscayne Bay. As photos of the stranded baby grand went viral, many people claimed credit for the stunt, but it turned out to be the work of 16-year-old student Nicholas Harrington. Nicholas hoped that photos of his piano prank would impress admissions officers at The Cooper Union college in New York City.

Call the Doctor!

Uplifting Story

Suan Jianhua feared he would never have a girlfriend because he suffers from a rare skin disorder called cutis laxa, which means his skin hangs in wrinkled folds. The 29-year-old from China looked like an elderly man after developing the condition when he was seven. Now, thanks to his family, who saved enough for a face-lift operation, Jianhua looks his true age and hopes to find love.

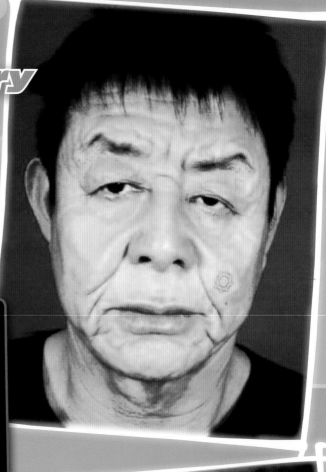

Supersize Stone

Kidney stones can cause agonizing pain. Most of them range in size from a grain of sand to a golf ball, so doctors were stunned when an X-ray revealed a stone the size of a coconut in a man's abdomen. Sandor Sarkadi from Hungary was rushed to the operating room where the stone, weighing almost two and a half pounds, was removed.

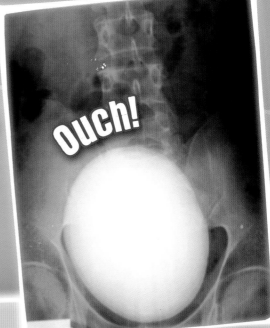

OUCH!

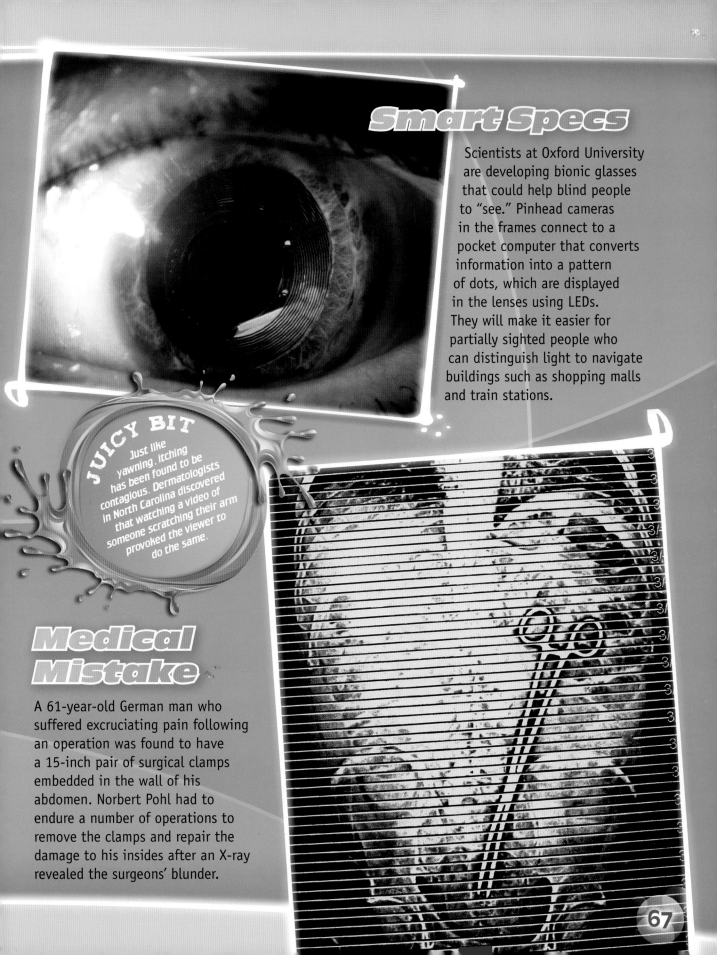

Smart Specs

Scientists at Oxford University are developing bionic glasses that could help blind people to "see." Pinhead cameras in the frames connect to a pocket computer that converts information into a pattern of dots, which are displayed in the lenses using LEDs. They will make it easier for partially sighted people who can distinguish light to navigate buildings such as shopping malls and train stations.

JUICY BIT

Just like yawning, itching has been found to be contagious. Dermatologists in North Carolina discovered that watching a video of someone scratching their arm provoked the viewer to do the same.

Medical Mistake

A 61-year-old German man who suffered excruciating pain following an operation was found to have a 15-inch pair of surgical clamps embedded in the wall of his abdomen. Norbert Pohl had to endure a number of operations to remove the clamps and repair the damage to his insides after an X-ray revealed the surgeons' blunder.

Ripley's @ a glance

SEWAGE STEAK

Mississippi mud pie is a treat, but what about food made from real sewage mud? A Japanese researcher discovered that sewage contains a lot of protein, and he has developed a process for turning it into a meat substitute that apparently tastes like beef.

CLEVER CARTON

Designer Ko Yang has created a milk carton that gradually changes color from white to orange as the expiration date approaches, so there should be no need to sniff the milk to find out if it's sour.

PHONE FUN

Pre-history meets modern technology in a custom-made iPhone 4 that has a back made from a 65-million-year-old polished meteor stone with the tooth of a T. rex sculpted into the material. The device, created by British jeweler Stuart Hughes, also features a bezel of diamonds and a platinum Apple logo. The History Edition model retails for about $62,700.

Reportedly commissioned by an Australian businessman, the $3-million iPhone 3GS Supreme could be the most blingtastic iPhone case in the world. The screen is framed by 136 diamonds totaling 68 carats, and there are more diamonds on the solid-gold back. The Apple logo is pictured in another 53 diamonds and the navigation button on the front is a single 7.1-carat diamond.

Sales of C.J. Corporation's mini-sausages boomed during cold weather in South Korea when people found that they made perfect finger substitutes—users tapped on their phones with the sausages and were able to keep their gloves on!

WHAT NOSE?

You can see your nose all the time, even if it's not big, however your brain chooses to ignore it.

EARS AND i'S

While sketching ears when applying to art school, Daniela Gilsanz came up with this cheeky idea to disguise the fact that someone's on the phone. Her range of iPhone cases gives the perfect camouflage for a secret phone call. Smart phone-istas can choose from a selection of ear shapes and sizes, with or without sideburns, earrings, and piercings.

SILVER LINING

The Underfull tablecloth, created by Norwegian designer Kristine Bjaadal, turns clumsiness into art. It appears to be a traditional, white damask cloth, but when a colored liquid such as red wine is spilled on it, a hidden pattern is revealed.

YOUR INBOX IS FULL

During 2010, 1.9 billion Internet users sent a total of 107 trillion—that's 107,000,000,000,000—e-mails.

DISTANT DINOS

Timewise, we are closer to T. rex than this carnivorous dinosaur was to Stegosaurus. Tyrannosaurus lived from 67 to 65.5 million years ago in the Cretaceous period and Stegosaurus lived much earlier, during the Late Jurassic, 155 to 150 million years ago.

MUST-SEE TV

Semi-transparent LEDs that can be incorporated into contact lenses are being developed at the University of Washington. If the project is successful, the system will be able to project images from TV, movies, or games directly onto the lenses. And since the lenses are beneath your eyelids, it's no good shutting your eyes if things get too scary.

REVEALING DRESS

There's no hiding your true feelings in the Bubelle Dress, which changes color according to your mood. The inner layer of the dress contains biometric sensors that pick up a person's emotions and projects them as colors onto the outer layer.

YOUR PLANT TWEETED

People are known to talk to their plants, but soon the plants might talk back. While drooping leaves are a plant's normal way to say it's thirsty, students at New York University are working on a device activated by soil-moisture sensors that allows plants to tell owners when they need water—or if they've had too much—via Twitter.

MIND-BOGGLING

According to Google, the Internet holds about five million terabytes of data, which is five trillion megabytes. Based on an estimated capacity of five terabytes per human brain, it would take a million brains to store all the information on the Internet.

Home Sweet Home

Up, Up, and Away

It seems that Pixar's movie *Up* wasn't so far-fetched after all. A house with two people inside was attached to 300 eight-foot-tall helium weather balloons and launched from an airfield near Los Angeles as part of the *National Geographic* show *How Hard Can It Be?* The 16-square-foot house reached an altitude of 10,000 feet and was airborne for over an hour.

Now You See It...

Sarah and Philip Marsh fell in love with Coombe Trenchard as soon as they saw it. The early 20th-century house in southern England had hardly changed since its elderly owner had moved in 50 years earlier. Shortly after buying the property, they discovered a disappearing wall that slides down into the floor. Although it had not been lowered for decades, the mechanism still worked perfectly.

Safe as Houses

For anyone looking for maximum security, the Safe House, on the outskirts of Warsaw, Poland, is the ultimate panic room. At the touch of several buttons, the house closes up into an indestructible fortress as concrete panels and roller doors seal up the windows and entry points. Then the only way to get in and out is via a second-floor entrance protected by a drawbridge.

Big-Ticket Bedding

A store in Jiangsu Province, China, is selling a bedding set for one million yuan ($157,000). Based on royal bedding from the Qing Dynasty (1644–1911), the set includes a sheet, a bed cover, two quilt covers, and four cushions. It took ten people several months to create the handmade bed linen, which is decorated with a dragon and phoenix motif.

How much?

Medical Miracles

No H₂O

Many teenage boys give the impression that they are allergic to water, but in Ryan Clarke's case it's true. Ryan, who lives near London, England, is one of only 30–40 people in the world with Aquagenic urticaria, which makes his skin extremely itchy and painful whenever it comes into contact with water. Despite his condition, the schoolboy still showers daily.

Big Foot

Li Jinpeng from China was not only born with eight toes on each foot, he had a total of 15 fingers, too. Although this might have been useful for counting to 31, the six-year-old had trouble finding shoes to fit and was called a monster by some of his classmates, so he had a five-hour operation to remove the extra digits.

Little Linguist

When three-year-old Dimitrije Mitrovic from Serbia woke up speaking English, his family was mystified because he had never been taught the language. By the time he was five, Dimitrije was reciting *Harry Potter* novels and at the age of 11 he could speak the language like a native. He dreams in English and only reverts to his mother tongue if he is forced to.

JUICY BIT
People with hexadactylism have six fingers or toes. The condition affects about five babies in every 10,000 and often runs in families. It is very common for the extra digits to be soft tissue only, with no bones, and no function at all.

Pint-sized Teen

Junrey Balawing celebrated turning 18 with a drink in a glass that was almost as big as he is, because Junrey measures just 23.5 inches tall. He lives in a remote region of the Philippines with his family, who are all of normal height. His mother says he stopped growing after his first birthday and has remained the same size ever since.

Animal Magic

Who's the Human?

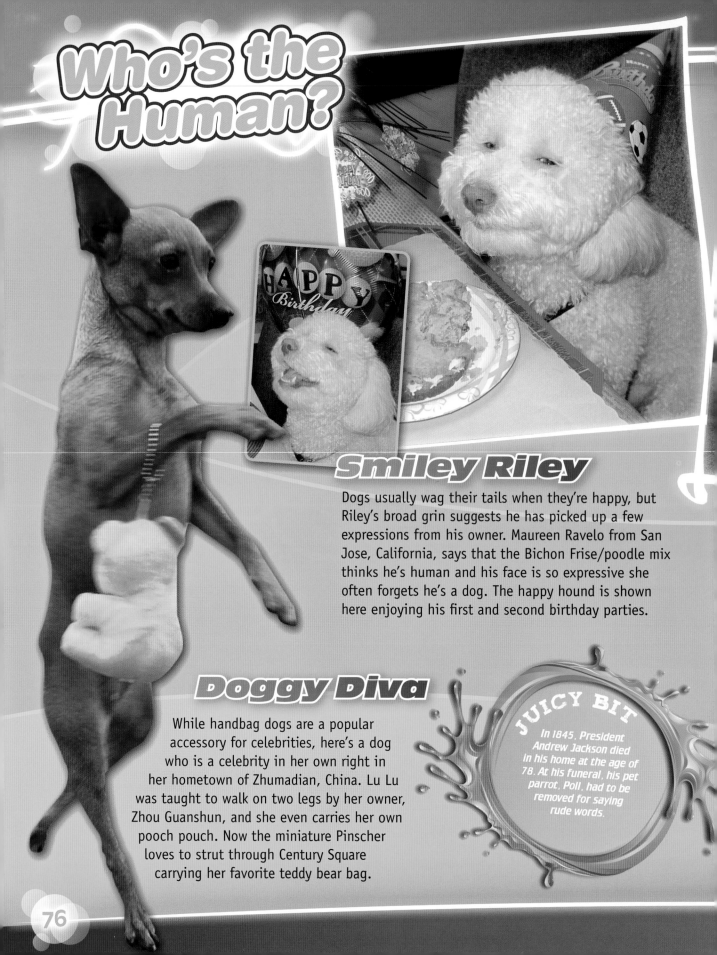

Smiley Riley

Dogs usually wag their tails when they're happy, but Riley's broad grin suggests he has picked up a few expressions from his owner. Maureen Ravelo from San Jose, California, says that the Bichon Frise/poodle mix thinks he's human and his face is so expressive she often forgets he's a dog. The happy hound is shown here enjoying his first and second birthday parties.

Doggy Diva

While handbag dogs are a popular accessory for celebrities, here's a dog who is a celebrity in her own right in her hometown of Zhumadian, China. Lu Lu was taught to walk on two legs by her owner, Zhou Guanshun, and she even carries her own pooch pouch. Now the miniature Pinscher loves to strut through Century Square carrying her favorite teddy bear bag.

JUICY BIT

In 1845, President Andrew Jackson died in his home at the age of 78. At his funeral, his pet parrot, Poll, had to be removed for saying rude words.

"Take a seat!" might be a more appropriate command than "Sit!" when Irish wolfhound Druid visits the Allambie Veterinary Clinic in Sydney, Australia. Other dogs are happy to sit on the waiting room floor, but this gentle giant perches on a chair next to his owner, Pamela Mullan. Since taking up the habit, he has started sitting in the car like a human passenger, too.

Designer Doghouse

This $400,000, architect-designed pooch palace in Gloucestershire, England, is home to two pampered Great Danes. The dogs have their own rooms with sheepskin-lined, temperature-controlled beds, and automatic dispensers that provide chilled water and deluxe food. Other luxuries include a spa bath and a 52-inch plasma TV—and in case their canine neighbors get jealous, there's a retinal scanner at the door to keep out unwanted guests.

Good Sports

Over the Moon

Regina Mayer's parents wouldn't let her have a horse, so the 15-year-old from Bavaria, Germany, decided to train the family cow to make her show-jumping dreams come true. It took the determined teenager two years to teach Luna to gallop and jump fences, spurred on by carrots. The clever cow has now learned several commands and can clear obstacles over three feet high.

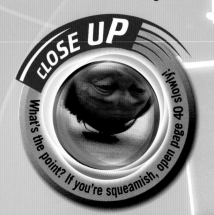

CLOSE UP

What's the point? If you're squeamish, open page 40 slowly!

Bunny Hopping

Rabbits love to hop, so perhaps it's not surprising that their natural behavior inspired a new sport. Rabbit jumping began in Scandinavia and has since become popular around the world. The ideal jumping rabbit has long legs and a long back. Champions can clear obstacles that are over three feet high, and cover close to ten feet in the long-jump competition.

Weighing in at just over two pounds, Nancy the chihuahua loves herding sheep that are ten times her size. Her owner said that the tiny rescue dog has a natural ability and learned by watching other sheepdogs at work.

Goats Defy Gravity

Alpine ibex goats enjoy a challenge and this plucky herd is no exception. The death-defying mountain goats regularly scale the near-vertical 160-foot Cingino Dam in the Italian Alps to eat the moss and lichen off the stones, and to lick the salts off the dam wall. The salts are rich in minerals that are lacking in the ibexes' regular diet.

Pigs Might Fly

Scarlett, a trampolining pig, had high hopes of stardom when her owners, Steve and Gwen Howell from Shropshire, England, entered her in a British TV talent contest. The rare-breed piglet's secret skill was discovered when they put her on their daughters' trampoline and found that she loved it. Now the girls have to wait their turn until Scarlett has finished jumping.

Boing!

Ripley's @ a glance

HUNGRY GATE-CRASHER

Luckily, wildlife photographer Andy Rouse had his camera in his hand when a polar bear popped his head through the kitchen porthole of a tourist ship in the Arctic. The hungry bear was attracted by the smell of lunch cooking.

CICADA SWARM

In May 2011, millions of cicadas filled the air in the southern United States as they completed their 13-year life cycles. Periodical cicadas spend most of their lives underground as nymphs before emerging to mate. The inch-long insects are harmless but annoying, as they get in people's hair, cars, and houses, and the males are ear-splittingly noisy when they sing to attract females.

RESCUE DOG

A dog saved the life of an abandoned newborn baby by keeping her warm among its litter of puppies on a cold winter's night near La Plata, Argentina. Farmer Fabio Anze found the baby among the puppies the following morning.

VIRAL VIDEO

A YouTube video showing wolves running wild through downtown Moscow, Russia, quickly became an online hit. The pack charged toward a policeman who had just flagged down a car with a faulty headlamp, causing him to leap into the passenger seat. However, it turned out to be a spoof for a viral marketing campaign promoting a drink with a wolf's-head logo.

TAKEN ON BOARD

Domingo Pianezzi makes a point of training his furry friends to ride the waves with him. He's shared a board with parrots, hamsters, even an alpaca, a creature from his native Peru. Here, he's managed to convert a usually water-shy cat to be a willing boarding buddy.

FIN DOCTOR

Ornamental fish enthusiast Patit Paban Halder has set up a hospital for fish at his home in Chandannagore, India. The hospital has 32 aquariums where he cares for sick fish, checking them for fungal and bacterial infections, and even giving them shots to make them better.

GENTLE GIANT

Keepers at Pocatello Zoo, Idaho, were worried when Shooter, a ten-foot-tall elk, started to behave strangely at his water trough. All was explained when he lifted a tiny woodchuck from the water and gently nudged it with his hoof to make sure it was still alive. The lucky woodchuck quickly scampered off into some nearby bushes.

BRILLIANT BEASTIES

Gorillas can catch colds and flu from humans, and they are more likely to die from these diseases because their immune systems can't cope with them.

If you see a spotted skunk doing a couple of handstands, keep clear—it's about to spray.

A wild lion normally makes a maximum of 20 kills a year.

Caterpillars have about 4,000 muscles compared to humans, who have just 629. An average garden caterpillar has 248 muscles in its head alone.

A male woodpecker may strike a tree up to 12,000 times a day, but it doesn't get a headache because its thick skull is made of spongy bone that cushions the blows.

Scallops have up to 100 eyes that detect light and motion.

China is home to half of the world's pigs.

According to a law, in Alaska it is illegal to whisper in a person's ear while they are moose hunting.

It is said that if a small amount of rubbing alcohol is put onto a scorpion's back, it will sting itself to death.

Although the lion is known as the king of beasts, it would be easily defeated by a polar bear in a fight between the two.

FAST FOR FREEDOM

When Jake the Jack Russell terrier vanished during a walk, his owners, Rick and Jill Thomas from South Wales, had no choice but to return home without him. Twenty-five days later he turned up at a local farm in a terrible state. A veterinarian concluded that the well-fed dog had gotten trapped in a rabbit hole and only managed to escape once he had lost enough weight to wriggle free.

ODD INT-ROO-DER

When an intruder burst through their bedroom window, Australian chef Beat Ettlin and his wife thought they were being robbed until the shadowy figure started bouncing on their bed. Then they realized that the housebreaker was a kangaroo. Mr. Ettlin jumped on the 90-pound marsupial and managed to wrestle him out the front door.

Behave!

Steer Gets Stuck

An inspector from a Scottish animal charity rescued a steer in South Ayrshire, Scotland, after members of the public spotted the Belgian Blue bullock with its head wedged between the rungs of a ladder. Inspector Kerry Kirkpatrick managed to ease the ladder off the steer's head and return it safely to the herd.

You Looking at Me?

JUICY BIT

A pet cat was summoned to report for jury duty at a Boston court. Although his owner, Anna Esposito, explained that Sal was unable to speak and understand English, the court insisted that he attend.

A chicken farmer from Xiamen, China, came up with a novel way to stop his roosters from fighting. Zhang Xiaolong was losing up to ten birds a day in fights, so he equipped his flock with glasses. Unlike most spectacles, instead of helping the birds to see, they stop them from looking straight ahead, so they can't make eye contact with one another and start a fight. This idea isn't new, however: A 1951 British Pathé newsreel featured chickens wearing spectacles, calling them a "cure for hen pecks."

ZZZZZZ...

Caught Napping

Lots of creatures enjoy a nap after a meal, but it's not often you catch a bird taking a snooze. Wildlife photographer Ian Butler was doubly delighted to capture this woodpecker dozing on a branch because it was also the first time he had managed to photograph the shy bird. The woodpecker had been feasting on ants in an orchard in the Malvern Hills, central England.

CLOSE UP

Look what's kicking off on page 58!

Hello DJ Kitty

Every common kitten feels the need to sharpen their claws on a scratch mat, post, or something similar, but cool cats today spin the decks as they do it. This Cat Scratch in the shape of a turntable comes complete with a movable stylus arm and a spinning record.

BIG SHOT

Dogs in Disguise

The canine contestants that take part in America's extreme dog-grooming contests may arrive looking like poodles, but two hours later they are totally transformed—often into completely different creatures. The groomers can dye the fur of their dogs before the competition, but the final styling is done during the show. Luckily, the dogs seem to enjoy all the pampering and attention as they are sculpted into horses, lions, zebras, pandas, or even people.

Yeehah!

Groomers are allowed to use costumes, props, and music to complete the transformation of their poodle partners.

Gene Genius

Real Sheep Dog?

Thousands of people flocked to Liu Naiying's farm in Shaanxi Province, China, after the farmer claimed that one of his ewes had given birth to a puppy. The "puppy" has wool like a lamb but its head, paws, and tail look more like a dog's. Liu took the newborn creature home because the ewe refused to feed it, and says that the animal behaves just like a dog.

JUICY BIT

The ridged pattern on a cat's nose pad is unique—no two are alike, just like human fingerprints. Cats also use their noses for detecting temperature changes as well as for smelling.

Head Turner

A calf with two heads was born at a farm in Hebei Province, China. The heads are both fully formed, but they share three ears. Farmer Dong Yubao's wife was helping with the birth and collapsed when two heads and four eyes emerged. The calf cannot stand by itself so it has to be bottle-fed with sheep's milk.

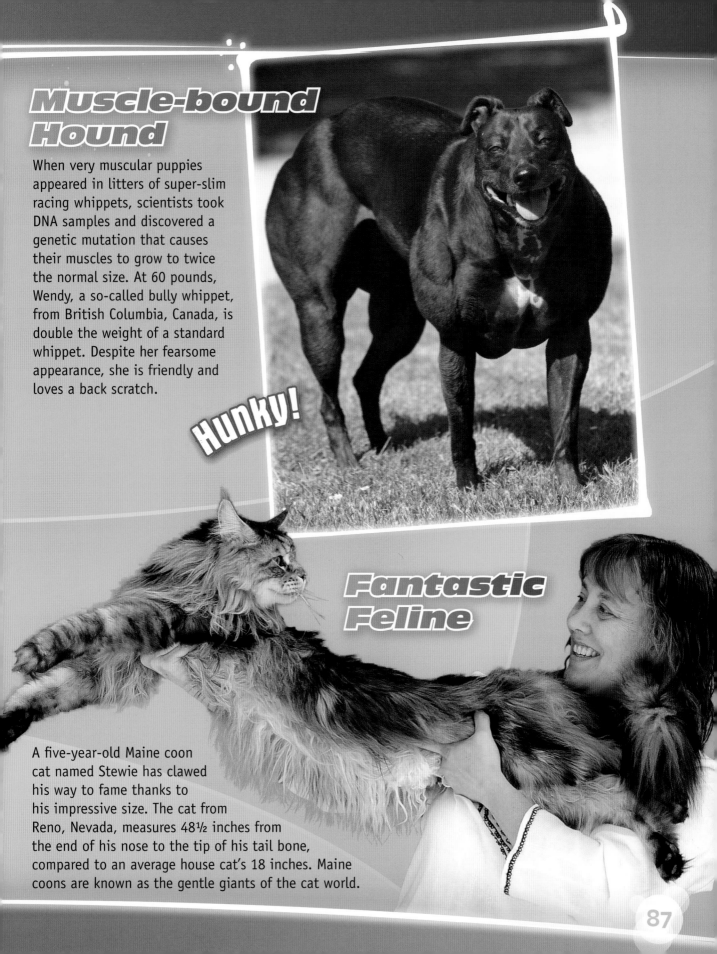

Muscle-bound Hound

When very muscular puppies appeared in litters of super-slim racing whippets, scientists took DNA samples and discovered a genetic mutation that causes their muscles to grow to twice the normal size. At 60 pounds, Wendy, a so-called bully whippet, from British Columbia, Canada, is double the weight of a standard whippet. Despite her fearsome appearance, she is friendly and loves a back scratch.

Hunky!

Fantastic Feline

A five-year-old Maine coon cat named Stewie has clawed his way to fame thanks to his impressive size. The cat from Reno, Nevada, measures 48½ inches from the end of his nose to the tip of his tail bone, compared to an average house cat's 18 inches. Maine coons are known as the gentle giants of the cat world.

Life Savers

Goal-fish

After storms hit Cumbria, northwest England, two goldfish were found stranded in puddles of floodwater on a soccer field. Emma Story, the soccer club owner's daughter, who was helping with the cleanup, popped them in a mop bucket. The club kept the fish as mascots until 2010 when one of them died.

Dog Guides Dog

JUICY BIT

Tami Akanuma is convinced that her dog saved her life after the 2011 earthquake and tsunami in Japan. Babu insisted on going for a walk up a nearby hill minutes before the devastating tsunami swept through their home.

Graham Waspe from Stowmarket, England, was devastated when his guide dog, Edward, lost his sight because of inoperable cataracts after six years of loyal service. Mr. Waspe, who has lost one eye and has limited vision in the other, wanted to keep Edward as a pet, so his guide-dog successor, Opal, now helps both the blind dog and his master to get around.

Panda Parents

Chinese conservationists are going to extreme lengths to prepare their captive-born panda cubs for life in the wild. It's vital that the cubs have as little human contact as possible, so researchers dress up in fluffy panda costumes whenever they need to handle them. With fewer than 3,000 pandas left in the wild, the captive-breeding program at the Hetaoping Research and Conservation Center in western China is the best hope of saving the endangered species.

Double Takes

Cunning Disguise

Fish swim in schools for protection against predators, and a huge school of sardines seems to have taken this instinctive behavior a step further by disguising themselves in the shape of a huge predator. Belgian photographer Steve De Neef, who captured the dolphin-shaped school in the Philippines, said he was sure it was a coincidence, but it would definitely benefit them to imitate a larger animal.

Undercover Facts

The word "camouflage" is derived from the French word *camoufler* meaning "to blind or veil."

During the 1991 Gulf War, the military used toilet paper to camouflage their tanks in the Saudi Arabian desert.

Americans during World War II used a technique called Razzle Dazzle in which complex geometric patterns were painted on battleships to break up their lines and angles so they were less identifiable to the enemy.

To ward off enemy fire, Burbank's Lockheed Air Terminal (now called Bob Hope Airport) was entirely covered with strategically placed camouflage netting during World War II. From the sky, and to the enemy, the whole area looked like a rural landscape.

Woof!

Canine Creation

Hair and chewing gum are not normally a good mix, but Gareth Williams made use of these recycled materials in his unique sculpture *I Say, I Say, I Say*. The dog-shaped model is formed from pre-chewed gum and the artist's own hair clippings. The artwork was showcased at an exhibition for graduate sculptors at the Royal College of Art in London, England.

Pucker Up

One day when she was bored, Paige Thompson came up with the idea of painting animals on her mouth with leftover Halloween face paints. The body-paint artist from Texas started with a bumblebee, then a fox, and as her animal collection increased she christened them "Animal-ipsticks." It takes Paige half an hour to paint each creature in her mouth menagerie.

JUICY BIT

British art college graduates Azusa Murakami and Alexander Groves have come up with a clever use for a renewable resource. "Hair Glasses" are biodegradable spectacle frames made of human hair trimmings bound with bioresin.

Sharp Survivors

Many animals use mimicry or camouflage to fool predators, and thorn bugs are real masters of disguise. These prickly tricksters are members of the treehopper family and feed on the sap of their host tree or bush. By mimicking spiky thorns on a branch, they are able to confuse birds and other predators that would otherwise eat them.

Homing Instinct

Domesticated Deer

Dillie the deer was rescued by Dr. Melanie Butera, a veterinarian from Ohio, after being abandoned by her mother. The family's poodle and Melanie's husband, Steve Heathman, took Dillie under their wing and the deer now climbs stairs, turns lights and faucets on and off, and takes ice from the refrigerator dispenser. Dillie enjoys lounging on the bed and swimming in the pool, and her favorite meal is pasta and ice cream.

Shlurp!

Bunny Babysitter

Koa the Labrador is taking care of two baby rabbits after discovering them while chasing a lizard. Her owner, Tina Case of San Francisco, says the baby bunnies hop all over the dog and always find their way to the crook of Koa's leg for warmth and shelter. The family plans to release the rabbits or give them to a nature reserve.

Cubs' Caregiver

A young chimpanzee called Dodo has become a substitute mom to a group of golden tiger cubs at a zoo in Bangkok, Thailand. The chimp gives the cubs bottles of milk, and has formed close bonds with his feline friends. Although Dodo loves to play with the baby tigers, keepers say that they will soon outgrow him, and then they will have to be separated.

JUICY BIT

Mia, a Belgian Malinois dog, miraculously survived a blaze that destroyed her owners' house by opening four doors and climbing into a basement bathtub. As firefighters fought the flames, water filled the tub and kept Mia safe.

Roaming Reptile

When Phillipa Durrant ordered a belt from eBay, she was shocked to find something extra in the parcel. Sahara, a leopard gecko, had sneaked into the package after it was left close to his tank. While his owners in Birmingham, England, were busy searching for him, Sahara was hitching a 100-mile ride to Finchampstead in Berkshire. The gecko was returned to his owners by special courier.

Big and Bold

Bad Dog

Family pet Si Mao knew she was in trouble after wolfing down her owners' lunch, so she went to lay low next door at Wuhan Zoo in central China—where she found the perfect hiding place behind lioness Zhen Zhen! A spokesman for the zoo said the dog was lucky she hadn't chosen the tigers, otherwise she would have been lunch herself.

Cat City

Craig Grant didn't even like cats when his son moved out of their home and left his cat behind. But when the cat gave birth to kittens, and Craig's feline family grew, he decided to build a more suitable home for them, and founded Caboodle Ranch in Florida. The 30-acre sanctuary, with cat-sized buildings including a city hall and police station, is now home to 660 cats, and Craig has since become a confirmed cat lover.

Welcome Aboard

Whale watchers got a closer view than expected when a southern right whale leaped aboard their boat, snapping the mast in two. Paloma Werner and Ralph Mothes had been watching the whale near Cape Town, South Africa. Southern right whales have poor eyesight and navigate by sound, and as the boat's engine was off, the whale probably wasn't aware that it was there.

"Let's Talk"

Paloma, describe how it happened.
The whale first breached 400 yards away, then again at 200 yards. I was watching it from the side of the boat the whale landed on, but Ralph thought it had moved through the water to the other side, so he told me to move to see it. I'm glad I did. Suddenly I heard him call out and I looked behind me to see the whale rising up about 30 feet and land. It was like slow-motion. The mast came down, then the sails. I checked we were not taking on water and started the engine. We would have sunk if the boat had been fiberglass and not steel.

I was about six feet away from where the whale landed and if I had been standing in my original position I would have been killed. If it had happened one second later, it would have crashed onto the boat's coach house that we were standing in.

Was the whale hurt?
There were bits of skin and blubber left behind but no blood, so we have been assured by professionals that the whale will have recovered.

chapter 5

Fine Art

Take a Second Look

Real Talent

This image looks as if it had been snapped in a second, but closer inspection reveals that it isn't a photo, it's a hyperrealistic painting. It takes Denis Peterson a month of long days working to complete his paintings, which sell for up to $50,000. The New York artist blows up photographs 2,000 times to show every tiny detail before re-creating the image. His work ranges from street scenes to portraits of people around the world.

Carved from Wood

Randall Rosenthal carves objects from a single piece of wood, then paints them using *trompe l'oeil* ("deceive the eye") techniques. He chooses to paint items made from paper because paper is produced from wood. The East Hampton artist's box of "$100 bills" took 12 weeks to carve and paint, and later sold for $25,000 in real money, while his pile of "newspapers" announcing President Barack Obama's election is now in the White House.

Interactive Art

These incredible 4-D paintings on display at a Chinese art exhibition use clever shading to trick the eye into believing that the images are leaping off the canvas. Visitors become part of the artwork as they interact with the pictures—sitting on Pinocchio's nose, catching a fish from the mouth of a bear, or milking a cow.

JUICY BIT

Since 1974, German artist Peter Dreher has painted the same empty glass in the same position over 4,400 times. He says that although viewers may think the paintings are all the same, each reveals something different about the glass.

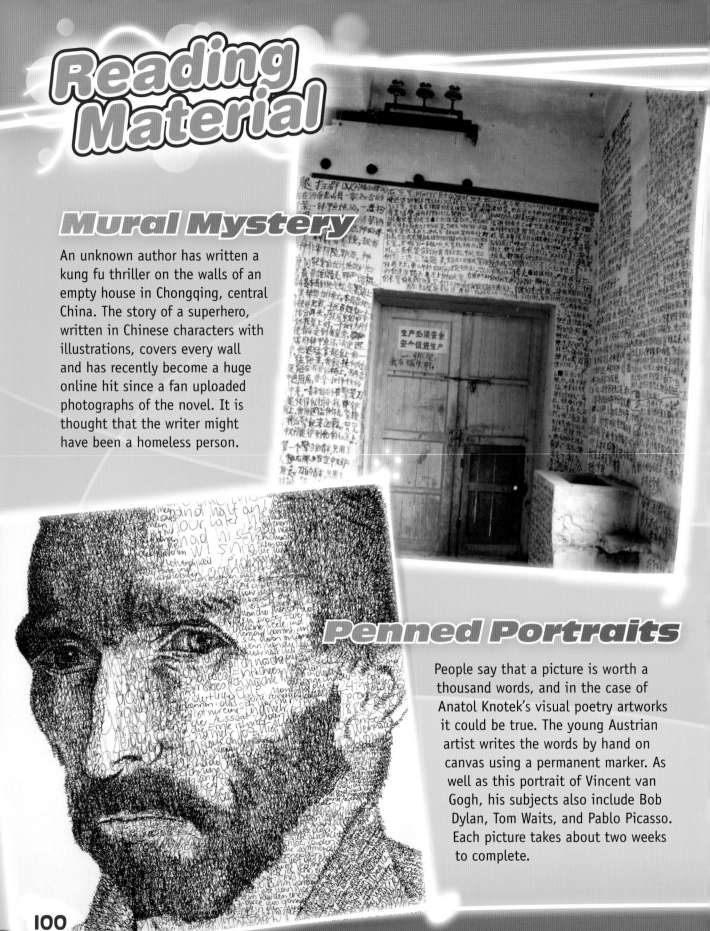

Reading Material

Mural Mystery

An unknown author has written a kung fu thriller on the walls of an empty house in Chongqing, central China. The story of a superhero, written in Chinese characters with illustrations, covers every wall and has recently become a huge online hit since a fan uploaded photographs of the novel. It is thought that the writer might have been a homeless person.

Penned Portraits

People say that a picture is worth a thousand words, and in the case of Anatol Knotek's visual poetry artworks it could be true. The young Austrian artist writes the words by hand on canvas using a permanent marker. As well as this portrait of Vincent van Gogh, his subjects also include Bob Dylan, Tom Waits, and Pablo Picasso. Each picture takes about two weeks to complete.

Stylish Threads

A photography student and fashion fan from Kingston University, England, has painstakingly cross-stitched three Vogue fashion magazine covers, each taking 50 hours. Inge Jacobsen stitched directly onto the cover after making holes through the paper, and she allowed the background to show through as part of the design. Her aim was to take something mass-produced and transform it into a unique work of art.

CLOSE UP

See page 45 for this high-drama chain reaction.

Eye-catchers

Canadian makeup artist Katie Alves re-creates scenes from everyone's favorite movies on her own eyelids using regular cosmetics. Her designs include landscapes from *The Lion King*, *Tangled*, and *Aladdin*, and each eye can take between one and two hours to complete. Unfortunately, the only way Katie can see her unusual artwork properly is by looking at a photo.

Caught on Camera

You've Grown!

Young Me/Now Me invites people to dig out old photos and re-create snapshots from their childhood down to the smallest detail. The participants pose in similar locations, matching their clothes, props, and facial expressions as closely as possible to the originals, often with amusing results. The project is the brainchild of Ze Frank, who is publishing the best photos in a book.

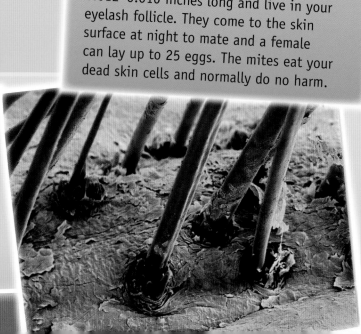

Micro Worlds View

Photographs from a book called *Microcosmos* show our everyday world in extreme close-up. Some of the subjects, which have been shot using electron microscopes, have been magnified 22 million times. This image shows human eyelash hairs at 50 times their actual size. Other photos include the tip of a hummingbird's tongue, bacteria, and the surface of a microchip.

Yuuukk!!

Did you know that about half of all people in the world have eyelash mites? They are 0.012–0.016 inches long and live in your eyelash follicle. They come to the skin surface at night to mate and a female can lay up to 25 eggs. The mites eat your dead skin cells and normally do no harm.

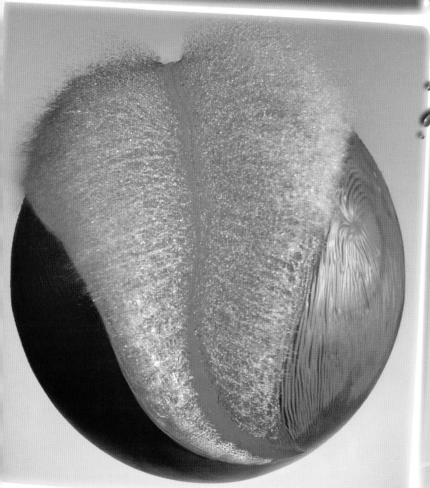

Pop Art

Working in his backyard at night and getting soaked are two of the hazards faced by Edward Horsford as he captures the moment when water balloons pop. He bursts the balloons with a long pin and the popping sound triggers the flash. The British photographer claims that bursting 30–50 balloons filled with dye leaves him looking like an abstract Jackson Pollock painting by the end of a shoot.

Bird's-eye View

Thrill-seeker Tom Ryaboi has pioneered a heart-stopping photography craze called "rooftopping." The travel photographer climbs to the top of skyscrapers and hangs off the edge to capture the perfect image. Tom developed his head for heights at the age of two, when he climbed onto the top of the fridge, and today he still feels compelled to sit on top of the tallest object he can see.

BIG SHOT

Hidden Talents

Waldo was easy to spot
compared to Liu Bolin—
the real-life invisible man.
Inspired by animals that
blend into their surroundings,
human chameleon Liu from
China disguises himself
to melt into any backdrop.
It takes up to ten hours of
painstaking work for Liu
to prepare for a photograph.
First he paints his clothing,
then he has to stand
completely still while
his assistants add the
finishing touches to his
perfect camouflage.

Where did he go?

Using nothing more than a few cans of paint, Liu performs spectacular disappearing acts worthy of any magician.

Artiful Art

Trash Transformed

This underwear, called *A Clean Pair for Every Day of the Week*, may look like something Lady Gaga might wear, but Ingrid Goldbloom Bloch's range of underwear woven from aluminum cans, rivets, dryer vents, and gutter guards is strictly sculpture. The American artist takes her inspiration from trash she finds on the street and interesting items she spots in hardware stores.

Subway to Starship

Hubert de Lartigue was fiddling with his Paris subway ticket between stops when he came up with the idea of recycling it into an X-wing fighter. Using just a scalpel and a folding tool, but no glue or paint, the French artist has created four different origami *Star Wars* ships and has shared the instructions on the Internet.

Green Theme

Artist Ju Duoqi used fresh, withered, rotting, dried, pickled, boiled, and fried cabbage to create sculptures of glamorous women for her project *The Fantasies of Chinese Cabbage*. Ju, from Beijing, China, started working with vegetables in 2006 and her past works include a portrait of Vincent van Gogh made from leeks and Napoleon on a potato horse.

JUICY BIT

Swedish furniture giant Ikea erected a huge silver birch tree sculpture laden with kitchen appliances outside the Barbican art center in London, England, in 2010 to mark their sponsorship of the center's Surreal House exhibition.

"Let's Talk"

Peter, how do you carve such complex shapes?
I've walked for weeks at a time in the Amazon jungle, in Southeast Asia, Africa, and New Guinea. At night, when it was too dark to walk or read, I would carve pencil-sized branches. In the dark, I'd have to carve by feel, rather than by sight, and so the helix and screw and spiral shapes were perfect. I'd twist the branch with one hand, holding my knife in the other, and I'd do that over and over again. So the shape formed!

So did you carry a bag of carved branches as you walked?
No, in the morning I'd climb a tree, bore a hole, and plant the branch I'd carved. If you're ever wandering around in the highlands of West Papua you might look up and see one.

Beautiful Bats

Peter Schuyff first started carving sticks for something to do in the evenings after walking in the jungles of New Guinea, the Amazon, and Burma. He continued after his return to New York, carving pencils in front of the TV. Now based in Amsterdam, The Netherlands, the artist sculpts intricate and twisting shapes from baseball bats.

107

Body Work

Ashes to Art

Daniel Ortega, who is based in Phoenix, Arizona, specializes in memorial ashwork—paintings created from the cremated remains of beloved pets. The tasteful tributes are full of color and decorated with jewels and stained glass—although some also incorporate horse manure and goat pellets. So far, most of the artist's paintings use pet remains, but he is eager to work with human ashes, too.

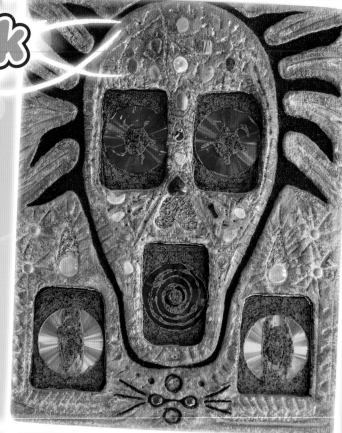

Navel-gazing

While resourceful artist Rachel Betty Case was at college, she realized that she could make art from anything. At first, she collected nail clippings, which she transformed into animal skeletons, then she moved on to another body by-product: belly button lint. She recycles what some people would consider a gross material to make cute teddies, which come in a black satin satchel so you can take them out and about. Rachel claims they are a great conversation starter.

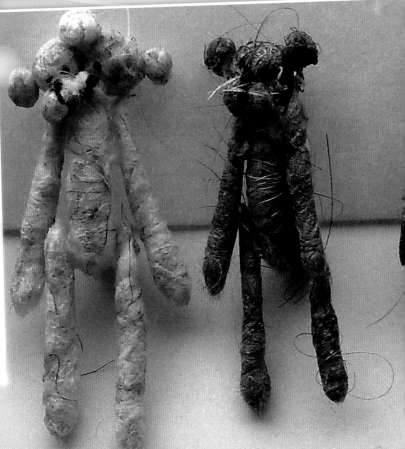

Crouching Tiger

Tigers are Craig Tracy's favorite animal, so the body-painting artist from New Orleans created this stunning piece of art to raise awareness of the critically endangered South China tiger. The 3-D image, which took 24 hours to complete, is painted on the bodies of three crouching people—the back of one forms the nose, while the eyes are drawn on the backs of the other two.

JUICY BIT
A video showing a man having a pair of glasses tattooed on his face became a YouTube sensation, but it was revealed to be the latest stunt in Ray-Ban's viral marketing campaign that included a cow giving birth to a man wearing sunglasses.

Portrait Gallery

Living Dolls

Boo Ritson paints people—literally. Her models are coated in layers of paint, then photographed before it dries, which gives them a plastic appearance. The British artist loves Americana, so her subjects include cowboys, cops, and cheerleaders, but also extend to fast food such as cheeseburgers and donuts. She allows 20 minutes to paint people, but spends 40 minutes on the burgers because they don't complain.

Paint-tastic!

Material Masterpiece

As a former fashion designer, Benjamin Shine was used to working with cloth, so he chose a single 26-by-10-foot length of black tulle to produce this homage to the great painter Rembrandt. The innovative artist from London, England, spent 200 hours scrunching, pleating, and pressing the fabric to depict the Dutch master of light and shadow.

Artistic Antics

Chris Trueman from Claremont, California, created a portrait of his six-year-old brother using 200,000 dead harvester ants. The artist originally tried to catch the ants by hand, but soon realized that he would have to buy them in bulk, so he ordered 40,000 at a time from a breeder who farms them as food for horned lizards.

Recycled Art

Glue-gunslinger Jason Mecier creates celebrity mosaic portraits from junk—often donated by the celebrities themselves. As a child, the San Francisco-based artist was told by his grandmother that he could make art out of anything. Now he tries to match the perfect items, colors, and themes to each subject, such as this patriotic portrait of President Barack Obama.

III

Ripley's @ a glance

DUST TO DUST

When most people see dust they reach for the vacuum cleaner, but for Paul Hazelton it is a valuable resource. The British artist, known as the Human Hoover, shapes moistened dust into 3-D sculptures, which include a moth, a briefcase, a human skeleton, and a complete miniature set of bedroom furniture.

PLASTIC PINKY

Matthew Tipler from Bend, Oregon, should always have his keys at his fingertips. When he lost the tip of his little finger, he had it encased in plastic and made it into a keychain.

TOOTHPICK TRANSPORT

Terry "Mr. Toothpick" Woodling has built a life-sized Wells Fargo stagecoach from 1.5 million toothpicks. It took the model maker from Warsaw, Indiana, 15 years to complete the coach and cost him over $1,200 in toothpicks alone. His previous model masterpieces include a locomotive (421,250 toothpicks), a Learjet (82,500 toothpicks), and a helicopter (8,500 toothpicks).

HOPPING MAD

Don't they look angelic? Look again. These cuddly looking bunnies are actually made from household waste, including Christmas tree needles, toenail clippings, human hair, and bits and pieces from discarded toys. It took Suzanne Proulx from Erie, Pennsylvania, 2½ years to collect enough dirt and dust to make 16 of her Dust Bunnies. She likes the thought of making something new from material that has been thrown away.

TATTOO TRIAL

After spending a full 52 hours under the needle, Nick Thunberg's body was left a bit sore, while his tattoo artist, Jeremy Brown, was exhausted and raw-fingered. The marathon tattoo session took place in Rockford, Illinois.

SLEEP PAINTER

A former nurse from Wales draws landscapes, figures, and portraits in his sleep, despite showing no artistic talent in his waking life. In his teens, Lee Hadwin drew on walls, furniture, or clothes while asleep, using anything that was nearby, including pieces of coal. Now the sleep-artist always keeps a sketchbook and pencils at hand.

BRUSH STROKES

The art world sometimes takes itself rather seriously, so here are a few fun facts about painters and paint.

Pablo Picasso's full name has 122 letters. The Spanish artist was baptized Pablo Diego José Francisco de Paula Juan Nepomuceno María de los Remedios Cipriano de la Santísima Trinidad Martyr Patricio Clito Ruíz y Picasso.

André Breton, founder of the art movement of Surrealism, came up with the anagram Avida Dollars (meaning "eager for dollars") as a nickname for Salvador Dalí, because he was jealous of the Spanish artist's commercial success.

In Leonardo da Vinci's day, women without eyebrows were considered more beautiful, which explains why the *Mona Lisa* has bare brows.

Southern California's South Coast Air Quality Management District estimates that drying paint releases more smog-forming fumes than all the area's oil refineries and gas stations combined.

CANVAS KISSES

Natalie Irish paints by kissing the canvas with her lipsticked lips. The young artist from Houston, Texas, varies the pressure of her kisses to create portraits of icons such as Jimi Hendrix and Marilyn Monroe. The idea first came to her as she blotted her lipstick on a tissue.

Labors of Love

Renaissance Rooms

From the outside, Robert Burns's rented home in Brighton, England, looks like an ordinary 1960s house, but the former decorator has transformed the interior in the style of Rome's Sistine Chapel. After spending his working life painting people's walls in boring pastel colors, the self-taught artist felt the need to get creative and copied Renaissance masterpieces from secondhand art books onto his own walls.

JUICY BIT

Singaporean artist Peter Zhuo, nicknamed Peter Draw, sketched caricatures nonstop for 24 hours to raise money for charity. He drew almost 1,000 people without eating or taking a break.

Oral Artwork

After being paralyzed following a wrestling accident, Doug Landis started to draw by holding a pencil in his mouth and discovered he had a hidden talent. Each picture takes the artist from St. Louis, Missouri, between 40 and 400 hours, and if it is a large piece he has to draw half the image upside down because of his limited reach.

Daily Bread

91 bowls of porridge

English designer David Meldrum, aka The Food Illustrator, has taken the food diary idea a step further by drawing everything he ate and drank each day for a year. The artist wanted the 365 images to be an honest snapshot, but admits that he sometimes chose food that had attractive packaging or would be better to draw—for example, a salad instead of curry. His diet included 1,360 cups of coffee, 122 chocolate bars, 34 packs of potato chips, 15 fried breakfasts, and 91 bowls of porridge.

15 fried breakfasts

David, what made you start the project?
I was sitting in front of a bowl of chicken noodles one evening, waiting for it to cool down. I started drawing it and thought what a good idea it could be to draw all I ate the next day, then I thought a week, a month...why not a year! Let's make it a real challenge.

Were there times when you thought you wouldn't complete it?
No. There were times when I got behind on the images and had to spend many late nights and weekends catching up, but, after committing myself, I had every intention of completing. The more followers I started to gain as the project went on, the more pressure there was to complete!

122 chocolate bars

What do you like best about the 365 pictures?
I like them being a complete collection that I hope will be interesting for people to see in years to come. In a hundred years' time, people can look back and say, "Wow! Look what they used to eat all those years ago!" The packaging and lettering included in the pictures will, I think, also show a part of history.

1,360 cups of coffee

34 packs of potato chips

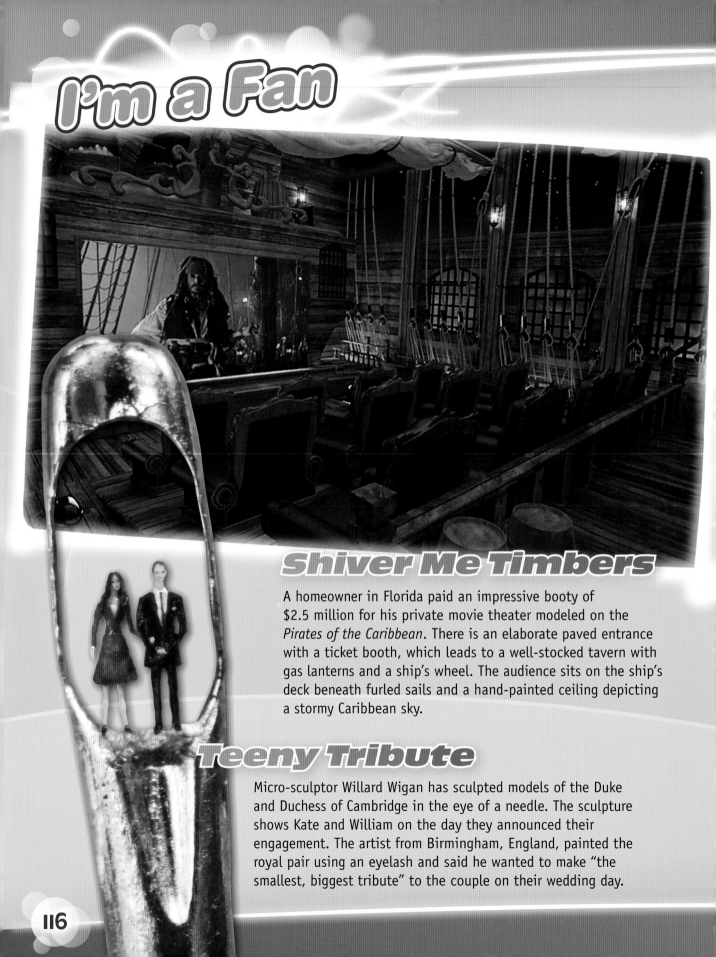

I'm a Fan

Shiver Me Timbers

A homeowner in Florida paid an impressive booty of $2.5 million for his private movie theater modeled on the *Pirates of the Caribbean*. There is an elaborate paved entrance with a ticket booth, which leads to a well-stocked tavern with gas lanterns and a ship's wheel. The audience sits on the ship's deck beneath furled sails and a hand-painted ceiling depicting a stormy Caribbean sky.

Teeny Tribute

Micro-sculptor Willard Wigan has sculpted models of the Duke and Duchess of Cambridge in the eye of a needle. The sculpture shows Kate and William on the day they announced their engagement. The artist from Birmingham, England, painted the royal pair using an eyelash and said he wanted to make "the smallest, biggest tribute" to the couple on their wedding day.

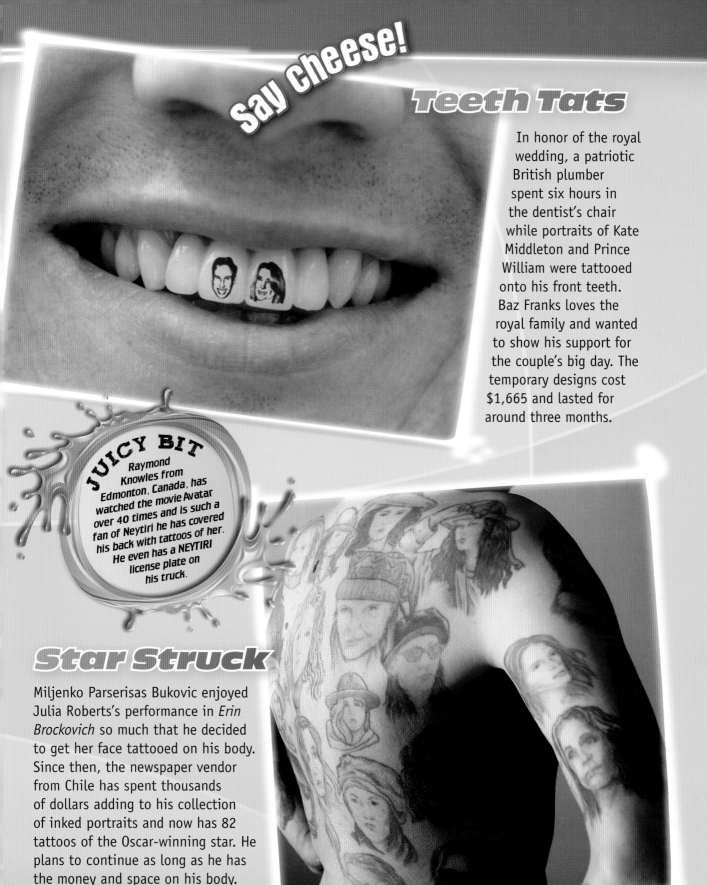

Say Cheese!

Teeth Tats

In honor of the royal wedding, a patriotic British plumber spent six hours in the dentist's chair while portraits of Kate Middleton and Prince William were tattooed onto his front teeth. Baz Franks loves the royal family and wanted to show his support for the couple's big day. The temporary designs cost $1,665 and lasted for around three months.

JUICY BIT

Raymond Knowles from Edmonton, Canada, has watched the movie Avatar over 40 times and is such a fan of Neytiri he has covered his back with tattoos of her. He even has a NEYTIRI license plate on his truck.

Star Struck

Miljenko Parserisas Bukovic enjoyed Julia Roberts's performance in *Erin Brockovich* so much that he decided to get her face tattooed on his body. Since then, the newspaper vendor from Chile has spent thousands of dollars adding to his collection of inked portraits and now has 82 tattoos of the Oscar-winning star. He plans to continue as long as he has the money and space on his body.

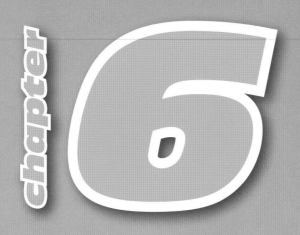

chapter 6

One in a Million

You've Changed

Epic Inking

Lake Jurosko from North Carolina is such a fan of the Disney movie version of *Alice in Wonderland* that she had the whole story tattooed on her back as a reward to herself for graduating from college. The elaborate design was a huge undertaking, and Lake endured inking sessions every other Saturday for the better part of a year.

JUICY BIT

To promote world peace, Har Prakash from New Delhi, India, has more than 300 national flags and 185 maps of countries tattooed on his body.

Queen of arts!

Pointed Smile

Members of the Mentawai tribe, from a cluster of islands off the coast of Sumatra, Indonesia, believe that women are more beautiful if they have their teeth chiseled to sharp points. This practice is part of the tribe's traditional culture that they still maintain today, and which also includes extensive body art.

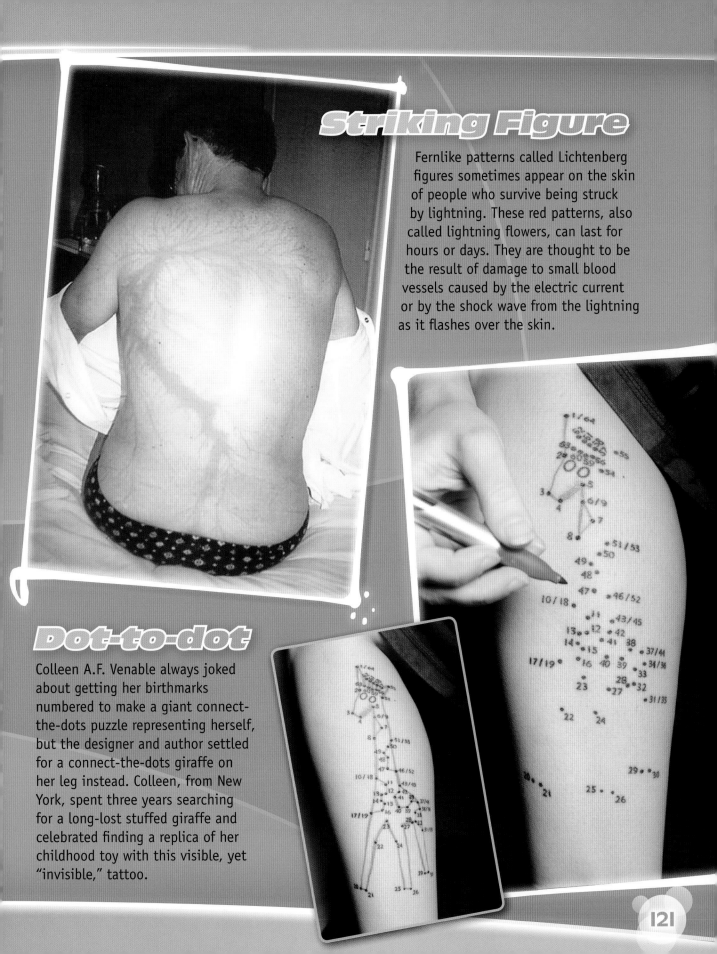

Striking Figure

Fernlike patterns called Lichtenberg figures sometimes appear on the skin of people who survive being struck by lightning. These red patterns, also called lightning flowers, can last for hours or days. They are thought to be the result of damage to small blood vessels caused by the electric current or by the shock wave from the lightning as it flashes over the skin.

Dot-to-dot

Colleen A.F. Venable always joked about getting her birthmarks numbered to make a giant connect-the-dots puzzle representing herself, but the designer and author settled for a connect-the-dots giraffe on her leg instead. Colleen, from New York, spent three years searching for a long-lost stuffed giraffe and celebrated finding a replica of her childhood toy with this visible, yet "invisible," tattoo.

More Anyone?

Chocol-art

Paul Wayne Gregory, from London, England, is an award-winning chocolate maker who puts the design into dessert by creating extraordinary sculptures. The real-life Willy Wonka starts by making a cast of the finished sculpture using a mold, then adds realistic details. His works include life-sized chocolate portraits, heads, and figures— and he accepts commissions if you have ever wanted to eat your own head.

JUICY BIT

According to the National Hot Dog and Sausage Council, based in Washington D.C., when kids were asked which condiment they would choose for their hot dog if their moms weren't watching, 25 percent said chocolate sauce.

Fancy Foods

Liven up your lunch box with this laser-engraved banana. Dutch company Studio:ludens has demonstrated its "Repper" pattern-producing software by adding geometric designs to boring bacon and bananas. The spokesperson explains why they want to add some pizzazz to more unfortunate foods: "Some of our food is given beautiful patterns by nature, like cauliflower and pineapples. Others, like the banana, have been less lucky."

Acquired Taste

Each spring, the air of Dongyang, China, fills with a foul stench as eggs are boiled in the urine of young boys, which is collected from nearby schools. The *Tong Zi Dan* (small boy eggs) have been a favorite street food in the eastern Chinese city for thousands of years, and local chefs are hoping that this special treat could soon become popular around the world. Lovers of the delicacy claim that the eggs stop fevers and help you concentrate if you're feeling sluggish or sleepy.

Work Wonders

George Black first picked up a field hockey stick at the end of World War II, and at 84 he still plays goal for his village team in Lanarkshire, Scotland. After becoming a goalie by accident, George soon became a legendary player in the world of Scottish field hockey and competed all over the globe. He now plays for the field hockey club Stepps fourth XI—sometimes against boys 72 years his junior.

Gifted Girl

Talented linguist Alexia Sloane fulfilled her dream of working as an interpreter at the European Parliament in Brussels, Belgium, despite being just ten years old and legally blind since the age of two. The schoolgirl from Cambridge, England, is fluent in French, Spanish, and Mandarin. She lost her sight because of a brain tumor, and was invited to Brussels after winning a Young Achiever of the Year award in 2010.

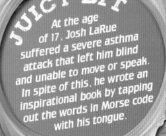

JUICY BIT

At the age of 17, Josh LaRue suffered a severe asthma attack that left him blind and unable to move or speak. In spite of this, he wrote an inspirational book by tapping out the words in Morse code with his tongue.

Guardian Angel

Police in Fribourg, Switzerland, hired a roadside angel to stop motorists driving too fast. A bearded actor dressed all in white played the angel, who stood at different locations around the 645-square-mile region, waving calmly at motorists and flapping his wings at speeding drivers. Drivers who spotted the angel were encouraged to e-mail the police, after which they were entered into a lottery for a free driving lesson.

Whoah!

Supple Sweeper

Zhang Xiufang became an Internet sensation after an iPhone video showing her performing exercises with her broom was uploaded to YouTube. The sanitation worker from Beijing, China, achieved overnight fame and was invited to appear on TV shows throughout the country. Her celebrity status cost her her day job, however, when she was fired because of her frequent absences from work.

CLOSE UP

Turn to page 80 for the animal on the crest of a wave.

BIG SHOT

Living Canvas

The Enigma has dedicated much of his adult life to covering every inch of his body with a jigsaw-puzzle tattoo, with as many as 23 tattoo artists working on him at one time. The body modification extremist from Seattle also has horn implants, reshaped ears, and a whole load of body piercings. So, he presents an awesome sight when he takes to the stage in the "Showdevils" tour, in which he stars, to perform stunts such as fire eating, sword swallowing, and hammering spikes into his blue head!

" I don't consider it a tattoo as much as just the color of my skin. Eventually I'll be all blue. This is the backside of the puzzle. The real art is on the inside. "

Tattooed Tales

Born in 1909, Betty Broadbent became one of the most famous tattooed ladies in American history. A woman with tattoos was an unusual spectacle at the time, and Betty traveled for more than 40 years with all the leading circus shows, where her good looks and sweet personality won the hearts of audiences around the world.

In the 1930s, in the Ringling Bros. Circus, Lady Viola had an all-body tattoo that included portraits of six U.S. presidents across her chest. The Capitol decorated her back, the Statue of Liberty and Rock of Ages decorated her legs.

The Ancient Greeks made a habit of tattooing the foreheads of their slaves with messages such as "Stop me, I'm a runaway."

In the late 19th and early 20th century, it was fashionable for aristocrats, including women, to be tattooed. Winston Churchill's mother, Lady Randolph Churchill, had a snake tattooed on her wrist.

Baby, You Were Born That Way

Shoulder to Shoulder

Joshua Carter from Leesburg, Georgia, can touch his shoulders together in front of his chest, but don't try this yourself. Joshua was born without collarbones, which means that he has hypermobile, or double-jointed, shoulders. The collarbone normally forms a strut between the shoulder blade and the breastbone, and is the only long bone in the body that lies horizontally.

"Let's Talk"

Joshua, does it hurt when your shoulders touch?
It actually does not hurt when my shoulders touch. Most people think that it does just because it is so abnormal. But it is just like touching your hands together.

Is your ability an advantage sometimes?
Having no collarbones is an advantage and a disadvantage. Without them it has allowed me to fit into small spaces and also work my way through a crowd very easily. But it also brings extra awareness, as that area is less protected without them.

As you have no collarbones, how do you keep your shoulders back?
My shoulders actually lean forward more than a normal individual. They are held up by my shoulder blades, but at the same time it is noticeable that my shoulders do sag forward without the added support.

Tomato Terror

A waitress from Southampton, England, is terrified of tomatoes. Kayleigh Barker loves ketchup, pizza, and pasta with tomato sauce, but cannot bear to look at a fresh tomato. Her fear, which is called Lycopersicon phobia, may date back to the time a friend filled her pockets with tomatoes and they got squashed.

Lid Licker

Moscow-born Nick Afanasiev, who now lives in California, can stretch his tongue to touch his lower eyelid, lick his nose and elbow, and even write text messages with its tip. Nick's tongue measures 3½ inches from the middle of his closed top lip to the tip. He owes his current acting career to his tongue, after being invited to show it off on TV shows.

JUICY BIT

Next time you're buying shoes, try measuring them against your forearm. The section between the elbow and the wrist is usually the same length as your foot.

Towering Teen

Elisany Silva has had to stop going to school because she is too tall to fit on the bus. At 6 feet 9 inches, the 14-year-old Brazilian girl towers over her classmates. Doctors think she is suffering from gigantism, a rare disease that causes extreme growth. Despite her problems, Elisany hopes to use her incredible height to her advantage by becoming a model.

Cool name, Les!

Perfect Pair

Two men who worked together at the Babeck Music Company in Olympia, Washington, in 1953 were clearly perfect partners. One was named Les Cool, and the other one was called Les Hot. Between them, they should have been able to achieve the perfect temperature!

Who's Wiser?

"Women are wiser than men because they know less and understand more," according to American humorist James Thurber, so he might have been interested to hear of a married couple who lived in Washington D.C. in 1941. The husband was called I.M. Wiser, while his wife's name was May B. Wiser.

Human Owl

Martin Joe Laurello entertained large crowds at Ripley's Odditoriums during the 1930s with his ability to turn his head back to front. Known as "The Man with the Revolving Head," the sideshow performer was born with a twisted spine that allowed him to walk forward while facing backward. When his head was turned, his spine formed the shape of a question mark.

BOO!

Long Locks

In 1937, Bertha Howard from Oregon personally wrote to Robert Ripley about her hair, which amazingly had grown to touch the floor. Her letter had been authenticated by John Gebbie, the Justice of the Peace in Prairie City, Oregon!

Dangerous Drop

Anyone stepping out of the door shown in this photo would have been faced with a long drop, because the front step is 18 feet above the sidewalk. The picture, taken in 1941, shows a building on the corner of Nichols and Dexter Avenues in Watertown, Massachusetts.

Tight Fit

A restaurant in Miami, Florida, was aptly named Hole in the Wall, because although it was 52 feet long, it was just 50 inches wide. The diner, which sold hamburgers and sandwiches back in 1948, was squeezed in between two stores, and was barely wider than the doorway.

It's a Gift

Tongue-tied

Florida resident Al Gliniecki served in the U.S. Navy, worked as a firefighter, won a wrestling championship, and was struck by lightning—twice—but perhaps his greatest achievement is that he can tie cherry stems into knots in his mouth. The paramedic's dexterous tongue can knot one stem in two seconds, 15 in one minute, 39 in three minutes, and (appropriately for a paramedic) 911 in an hour.

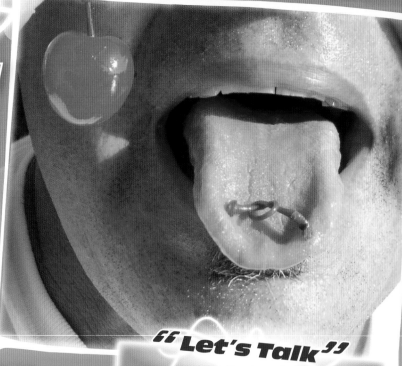

Eye-watering Stunt

Dong Changchun swallows small steel balls and makes them reappear from his eyes. The 50-year-old from Jinzhou, China, claims to use kung fu techniques to move the balls from his stomach back to his head, then he maneuvers them toward his eyes with a chopstick.

"Let's Talk"

Al, do you have a particularly unusual tongue?
No, my tongue is like everyone else's.

Explain your technique.
The length of the stem is really important. I prefer 1–1½ inches, and the thinner the stem the better. Thicker ones break a lot easier. Make sure the stem is at room temperature—if they are cold, like out from a cold drink, the stems seem to break faster. I use a four-step procedure:

1. I lay the stem across my tongue.
2. I close my mouth and turn my tongue sideways to cross the ends of the stem.
3. I push one of the ends through the circle with the tip of my tongue.
4. I spit the stem out.

Where does your talent go from here?
I have been practicing tying two stems together, two knots in one stem, and tying one Y-shaped stem into two knots.

The Tall Guy

In 2002, Canadian Doug Hunt walked 29 steps on carbon-fiber stilts measuring an incredible 50 feet 9 inches and weighing 137 pounds. Following that, in 2008, he organized a mass stilt walk with 625 students from his hometown of Brantford, Ontario, to benefit disabled people.

JUICY BIT

Laura Byng of Southend, England, drove bumper cars for 25 hours straight at the town's Adventure Island amusement park in 2011.

Real-life Rapunzel

Asha Mandela from Florida started growing her hair in 1988, and now her impressive dreadlocks measure an unbelievable 20 feet 1 inch. Asha needs a whole bottle of shampoo and conditioner to wash her hair, and it can take up to two days to dry. During the day, she usually wraps it in fabric and ties it to her back like a baby.

Ripley's @ a glance

I'M STUFFED

Adele Edwards eats cushions like candy. The Florida mom suffers from a rare eating disorder called Pica and has consumed the foam from seven couches over the past 21 years.

FEARSOME FANGS

The skull of a Viking warrior, unearthed from a burial pit on the south coast of England, revealed that the marauder had deep grooves filed into his two front teeth— probably to make him appear more ferocious to his enemies. The mass grave, discovered in 2009, contained 54 bodies, many of which had been beheaded.

LIFE SAVER

When two-year-old Mackenzie Argaet needed a liver transplant, the only option was to give her part of an adult liver, but its size meant that it was pressing against vital arteries. Her Australian surgeon came up with a novel solution and asked his wife to buy some Ping-Pong balls. He then inserted one between the new liver and Mackenzie's arteries to create a barrier. The ball is expected to stay there for the rest of her life.

DEAD INTERESTING

When American inventor Thomas Edison died in 1931, his last breath is said to have been sealed in a test tube, which is now on display at the Henry Ford Museum.

SLEEP YOURSELF SLIM

Couch potatoes may be surprised to learn that watching TV burns fewer calories than sleeping. Could this be because you can't snack in your sleep?

WHO'S @?

Celebrities come up with some unusual names for their children, but none so strange as the Chinese couple who wanted to call their baby @. When pronounced in English as "at," the symbol is said to sound like the Chinese for "love him."

UNLUCKY THIRTEEN

A 13-year-old boy was struck by lightning on Friday 13th at 13:13 in the afternoon. The boy, who was attending an air show in eastern England, only suffered minor burns and has since made a full recovery.

BACK FROM THE DEAD

Relatives of a Brazilian bricklayer got the shock of their lives when the man turned up at his own funeral. Ademir Jorge Goncalves had been mistakenly identified as the victim of a car crash.

HEADS UP

A human head is said to remain conscious for a short time after decapitation. People executed by guillotine during the French revolution were asked to blink afterward and continued to do so for up to 30 seconds.

Cockroaches can live without their heads for more than a week. They eventually die of starvation and dehydration.

There are about half a million people over 100 years old in the world, but only one in two billion will reach the age of 116.

Although more people are afraid of spiders than of dying, you are more likely to be killed by a champagne cork than by a poisonous spider.

When a beekeeper from the Spanish Pyrenees dies, his bees are all splashed with a drop of black ink.

Noted nutritionist Dr. Alice Chase, author of several books on healthy eating, died of malnutrition.

KICK START

Surgeons were operating on three-day-old Sam Esquibel to remove what they thought was a small brain tumor when a tiny foot popped out of his head. It is thought to have been a rare case of fetus in fetu, where a baby starts to grow inside the body of its twin.

BRAVEHEART

An Italian surgeon completed an operation to remove a brain tumor even though he himself developed a heart problem requiring emergency surgery partway through the procedure. Claudio Vitale refused to abandon his patient and finished the surgery before getting treatment himself.

Man and Machines

Mega Stretch

Why get a limo to take you to the party when you can party in the limo? The Midnight Rider is a 22-wheeler tractor-trailer limousine, 70 feet long and 13 feet high, which weighs a whopping 25.3 tons. With room onboard for 40 passengers, it is designed to re-create the feel of luxury rail travel and boasts three lounges, a full bar, and five TVs.

JUICY BIT

Auto fans can go out in style by taking the highway to heaven in a customized car casket. The fiberglass coffins by Cruisin Caskets of California have hinged tops and can be fitted with whitewall tires, and gold or chrome trim.

Front Room Ferrari

Ferrari fan Jon Ryder is so devoted to his 1996 Ferrari 355 Spider, he has converted his garage into a den so he can sit beside the car as he watches TV. The steelworker from Sheffield, England, has owned the vehicle for three years and admits that the novelty still hasn't worn off.

Before

One of a Kind

One of the world's wackiest watercraft began life as a Boeing 307 Stratoliner belonging to legendary industrialist and aviator Howard Hughes. After suffering hurricane damage, the plane was headed for the scrap heap until pilot Ken London bought it in 1969 for $62, cut off the wings and tail, and converted the fuselage into a motor yacht. Current owner Dave Drimmer bought the plane-boat for $7,500 and rebuilt the vessel, naming it the *Cosmic Muffin*. It is now available for charter in Fort Lauderdale, Florida.

After

PLANEBOATS.COM

A Question of Luck

Miraculous Escape

The driver of this Chinese truck cheated death after losing control of his vehicle on Heihe Bridge, in Changwu County, China. The truck flipped over the top of the barrier and was left dangling upside down over a 200-foot-deep gorge, suspended by just a single tire. Rescuers risked their own lives as they pulled the lucky man to safety.

Crane Crash

A crane operator escaped with just a few broken bones after the cab she was working in fell 300 feet from the top of a 33-story building in Leshan, southwest China. Construction workers were trying to raise the height of the crane when it tilted precariously. The control cab broke loose and plummeted down, leaving a large crater in the ground.

Hang in there!

Quite Shocking

A paraglider was left hanging by a thread when he became caught on power lines 100 feet above the ground in Switzerland. Rescuers could not touch the man because they would have sent thousands of volts coursing through his body, and the downdraft from a helicopter might have dislodged him. An inflatable mattress was brought in to catch him as he dropped, and he escaped without a scratch.

JUICY BIT

A truck driver from New Zealand was lucky to survive a freak accident when he fell onto a compressed air hose that pierced his body. Steven McCormack inflated like a balloon to twice his normal size.

Like Clockwork

Lowri Dearsley from Manchester, England, thought it was a timely coincidence when her second daughter, Evie, was born at 7:43 p.m. in December 2007 because her eldest daughter, Ella, had arrived at 7:43 a.m. in October 2005. Then in January 2011, baby Harrison entered the world—at 7:43 a.m. To mark the million-to-one chance, Lowri and her partner, Matt, both had 7:43 tattooed on their arms.

Index

Photo Credits

Ripley Entertainment Inc. and the editors of this book wish to thank the following photographers, agents, and other individuals for permission to use and reprint the following photographs in this book. Any photographs included in this book that are not acknowledged below are property of the Ripley Archives. Great effort has been made to obtain permission from the owners of all material included in this book. Any errors that may have been made are unintentional and will gladly be corrected in future printings if notice is sent to Ripley Entertainment Inc., 7576 Kingspointe Parkway, Suite 188, Orlando, Florida 32819.

FRONT COVER: Glen La Ferman

BACK COVER: Long hair—Asha Mandela; Foam sea—Bill Counsell; Longest tongue—Nick Afanasiev

CONTENTS PAGES: 2: Flip-flop monkey—Florentijn Hofman; Connect-the-dots tattoo—Joey Miller; **3:** Jumping from plane in chains—anthonyescapes.com; Touching shoulders together—Joshua Carter; Subway ticket origami—Hubert de Lartigue

INTRO PAGES: 4: Mechanical elephant—James Wigington; **7:** Jumping cow—Kerstin Joensson/AP/Press Association Images; The Enigma—Glen La Ferman; Where's Waldo—Con/Demotix/Demotix/Press Association Images

CHAPTER 1: 10: Bioluminescence—© Phil Hart/solentnews.co.uk; Guitar-shaped field—KeystoneUSA-ZUMA/Rex Features; **11:** Holland's striped fields—© EPA; Elephant rock—Richard and Ellen Thane/Science Photo Library; Juicy Bit—© freelancebloke - iStock.com (and throughout); **12:** Niagara Falls—© Vladone/istockphoto.com; Dry Niagara—Barcroft Media via Getty Images; Salt Lake—Massimo Brega, The Lighthouse/Science Photo Library; **13:** Giant drain hole far away—Carl McCabe; Giant drain hole close-up—John Terning; **14:** Rainbow clouds—© Caters News Agency Ltd.; Cloud spelling out "wish"—Daniele Siebenhaar/Rex Features; **15:** Frozen lighthouse—Lauren Jorgensen/AP/Press Association Images; Lighthouse unfrozen—Lisa Dejong/Landov/Press Association Images; Lightning strikes the Statue of Liberty—© Caters News Agency Ltd.; **16:** Church on a pillar—© Caters News Agency Ltd.; Egg house—jhphoto/AP/Press Association Images; **17:** Shed turned into diner—Paul Siudowski; Teapot building—CEN/Europics; **18:** Hot tarmac melts tire—Quirky China News/Rex Features; Car inside a van—CEN/Europics; **19:** 3-D girl crossing road—Wenn/BCAA Traffic Safety Foundation; Play-Doh car—Chevrolet/Rex Features; **20:** Painted mountain—© Jacques Sierpinski/Hemis/Corbis; Foam sea—Bill Counsell; **21:** Text box background image—© David Marchal - iStock.com; Burning crater—Dmitry Dudin; **22–23:** Flip-flop monkey—Florentijn Hofman; **24:** Miniature airport—Miniatur Wunderland/Rex Features; Tiny caravan—Jonathan Hordle/Rex Features; **25:** Indoor camping—Reuters/Tobias Schwarz; See-through airbus—© Airbus S.A.S.; **27:** Dolphin marriage—Israel Sun/Rex Features; **28:** Waving son off in pirate costume—Price Family/Rex Features; Manhattenhenge—KeystoneUSA-ZUMA/Rex Features; **29:** Skeleton drain—Wenn/Cem Ulucan; Aligator bike—Barcroft Media via Getty Images

CHAPTER 2: 32: Erupting volcano—© Caters News Agency Ltd.; Copper sulfate crystal house—Aisling Magill/Barcroft Media Ltd.; **33:** Freediver Carlos Coste—Dan Burton www.underwaterimages.co.uk; **34:** Wearing pink for 25 years—Austin Hargrave/Barcroft Media Ltd.; Boy wearing 215 pairs of underpants—Singer/Barcroft USA; **35:** 1250 copies of one novel—Quirky China News/Rex Features; Where's Waldo—Con/Demotix/Demotix/Press Association Images; **36:** Miniature art—www.aniskin.ru; Smallest Rubik's cubes—Evgeniy Grigoriev; **37:** Miniature computer parts—Yuri Zupancic/Solent News/Rex Features; Portraits of U.S. Presidents on hair—Sinopix/Rex Features; **38–39:** Jet bus—Indy Boys Inc; **40:** Headstand on a nail—Quirky China News/Rex Features; Floating vertically for 22 hours—Nagananda Swamy; **41:** Surf record—swell.com; Submarine—Sipa Press/Rex Features; **44:** Cable car hire

wire—Arno Balzarini/AP/Press Association Images; Alain Robert—Sipa Press/Rex Features; **45:** Jumping from plane in chains—anthonyescapes.com; **46:** Riding a log—Hiro Komae/AP/Press Association Image; Ashrita Furman—Reuters/Shannon Stapleton; **47:** Underwater marathon—Wolfgang Kulow; Lifting weights with teeth—© Akintunde Akinleye/Reuters/Corbis; **50:** Stunt Mini—© Caters News Agency Ltd.; Lorry that fell through bridge—CEN/Europics; **51:** Car driving on bottle track—Quirky China News/Rex Features; Cliff builders—CEN/Europics

CHAPTER 3: 54: Blood-scented perfume—Rex Features; LED teeth—wenn.com Creative Director, Art Director: Keiichi Uemura (SSF Tokyo), Production: amanainteractive inc.; **55:** Invisible coat—Shizuo Kambayashi/AP/Press Association Images; **56:** Creating static electricity with helicopter—Michael Yon; Bike printed from computer—Solent News/Rex Features; **57:** Duck-shaped boat—AFP/Getty Images; Crayola rockets—John Coker/Rex Features; **58:** Robot playing soccer—Reuters/Robert Pratta; **59:** Smartphone made out of paper—Queen's University/Rex Features; Paying with fingerprint—CEN/Europics; **60–61:** Photographed water droplets—Liquid Drop Art; **61:** Liquid drop art—Solent News/Rex Features; **62:** Cheating detector shin guards—© Caters News Agency Ltd.; Glasses for reading when lying down—Ray Tang/Rex Features; **63:** Japan's "Toylets"—Masatoshi Okauchi/Rex Features; Invention to propel inline skaters and skateboarders—Uwe Lein/AP/Press Association Images; **64:** UFO in China—CEN/Europics; Fruit fairy—Leon Schadeberg/Rex Features; **65:** Andy Sinatra—© 2005 Credit:TopFoto/Fortean Topfoto.co.uk; Mysterious piano appears in the middle of Biscayne Bay—Getty Images; **66:** Face lift transformation—CEN/Europics; Massive kidney stone—EPA/Photoshot; **67:** Glasses that restore sight—CEN/Europics; Surgery clamps left in stomach—CEN/Europics; **68:** iPhone ear cover—wenn.com; **70:** Balloon house—Wenn/Courtesy National Geographic Channel; Disappearing wall—Barry Gomer/Rex Features; **71:** The safe house—Aleksander Rutkowski- Robert Konieczny - KWK Promes; Expensive bedsheets—Quirky China News/Rex Features; **72:** Boy allergic to rain—Rex Features; Eight toes on each foot—CEN/Europics; **73:** Boy who woke up speaking English—CEN/Europics; Smallest man—Barcroft Media via Getty Images

CHAPTER 4: 76: Riley the smiling dog—Maureen Ravelo/Rex Features; Dog that walks upright—Quirky China News/Rex Features; **77:** Giant dog—Newspix/Rex Features; Luxury dog house—Rex Features; **78:** Show-jumping cow—Kerstin Joensson/AP/Press Association Images; Rabbit jumping—Action Press/Rex Features; **79:** Ibex on dam—© Caters News Agency Ltd.; Trampolining pig—NTI Media Ltd/Rex Features; **80:** Surfing cat—Pilar Olivares/Reuters; **82:** Cow with head stuck in ladder—Wenn/SSPCA; Special glasses for roosters—Xiang yang/AP/Press Association Images; **83:** Snoozing woodpecker—Ian Butler/Solent News/Rex Features; Cat DJ—Suck UK/Rex Features; **84–85:** Groomed poodles—Ren Netherland/Barcroft Media Ltd.; **86:** Sheep gives birth to puppy—Quirky China News/Rex Features; Cow with two heads—Quirky China News/Rex Features; **87:** Double muscle dog—© Stuart Isett/Anzenberger represented by: Eyevine; Longest cat—Andy Barron/AP/Press Association Images; **88:** Miracle goldfish—Owen Humphreys/PA Archive/Press Association Images; Guide dog with his own guide dog—Albanpix Ltd/Rex Features; **89:** Researchers dressed as pandas—Stringer Shanghai/Reuters; **90:** Sardines

in the shape of a whale—Steve De Nee/Solent News/Rex Features; Chewing gum dog—Getty Images; **91:** Animal lip art—Paige Thompson/Solent News/Rex Features; Camouflage thorn bugs—© NHPA/Photoshot; **92:** Dillie the deer—Melanie Butera, DVM; Dog that brought in rabbits—Tina Case/Rex Features; **93:** Chimpanzee feeds tiger cub milk—Sukree Sukplang/Reuters; Gecko that went on long trip—Ian Nicholson/PA Wire/Press Association Images; **94:** Dog hiding behind lion—CEN/Europics; Cat city—Rex Features; **95:** Whale jumping onto boat—James Dagmore/Polaris/Eyevine

CHAPTER 5: 98: Realistic painting—Barcroft Media via Getty Images; Wooden sculptures—Randall Rosenthal/Barcroft Media Ltd.; **99:** 4-D paintings—AFP/Getty Images; **100:** Thriller written on walls—CEN/Europics; Handwriting portraits—Anatol Knotek/Rex Features; **101:** Cross-stitched covers—Barcroft Media via Getty Images; Eyelid art—Katie Alves; **102:** Recreating old photographs—Ze Frank/Rex Features; Magnified eyelashes—Steve Gschmeissner/Science Photo Library; **103:** Bursting water balloon—Barcroft Media via Getty Images; Tom Rayobi—Wenn/Tom Rayobi; **104–105:** Camouflage art—Barcroft Media via Getty Images **106:** Tin can underpants—Dean Powell/Barcroft Media Ltd.; Subway ticket origami—Hubert de Lartigue; **107:** Cabbage portrait—Ju Duoqi/Solent News/Rex Features; Carved baseball bats—Peter Schuyff; **108:** Ash art—Daniel Ortega; **108–109:** Belly button bears—Chuck Nyce; Body art—Craig Tracy/Caters News; **110:** Air hostess art—Boo Ritson/Caters News; Light and shade fabric art—Benjamin Shine; **111:** Portrait made from ants—Chris Trueman/Rex Features; Ants—© Antagain - iStock.com; President Obama made from garbage—Jason Mecier/Rex Features; **112–113:** Dust rabbits—www.suzanneproulx.com; **114:** House that looks like the Sistine Chapel—Robert Burns of Brighton; Mouth art—Doug Landis; **115:** Food art—David Meldrum/Rex Features; **116:** Pirate-themed cinema—Elite Home Theater Seating/Rex Features; Royal couple in needle—NTI Media Ltd/Rex Features; **117:** Tooth tattoo of royal couple—SWNS; Julia Roberts Tattoos—Reuters/Eliseo Fernandez

CHAPTER 6: 120: Alice in Wonderland tattoo—Wenn/Hollyazzara.com; Chiseled teeth—Bob Huberman; **121:** Lightning mark—Image courtesy of the New England Journal of Medicine; Connect-the-dots tattoo—Joey Miller; **122:** Chocolate art—Multi-award-winning chocolatier Paul Wayne Gregory; Laser-etched banana—repperpatterns.com/Rex Features; **123:** Eggs cooked in urine—Quirky China News/Rex Features; **124:** 84-year-old still playing hockey—Alistair Devine/Rex Features; Youngest interpreter at the European Parliament—Geoffrey Robinson/Rex Features; **125:** Guardian angel of the road—© Europics; Sanitation worker exercises—wangchengbing/AP/Press Association Images; **126–127:** Glen La Ferman; **128:** Touching shoulders together—Joshua Carter; Phobia of tomatoes—M & Y Agency Ltd/Rex Features; **129:** Longest tongue—Nick Afanasiev; Tall teenager—Reuters/Paulo Santos; **132:** Knotting cherry stem in mouth—Alfred Gliniecki; Pushing steel balls through eyes—Quirky China News/Rex Features; **133:** Giant stilt walker—Brian Thompson; Long hair—Asha Mandela; **134:** Couch potato—© Chris Sadowski - iStock.com; **136:** Giant limo—www.themidnightrider.com; Ferrari in den—SWNS; **137:** Plane boat—David Drimmer; **138:** Lorry falling through bridge—Quirky China News/Rex Features; Crane crash—Quirky China News/Rex Features; **139:** Parachute caught in powerline—CEN/Europics/Rex Features; Three children born at the same time—Rachel Adams/Caters News